The $5 Dinner Mom One-Dish Dinners Cookbook

The $5 Dinner Mom
One-Dish Dinners
Cookbook

ERIN CHASE

ST. MARTIN'S GRIFFIN ❧ NEW YORK

www.stmartins.com

ISBN 978-0-312-61628-1 (trade paperback)
ISBN 978-1-250-01758-1 (e-book)

First Edition: September 2012

10   9   8   7   6   5   4   3   2

For all my fellow home chefs out there who need
a quick-fix healthy dinner

CONTENTS

ACKNOWLEDGMENTS

First of all, a heartfelt thanks to all my food testers. I appreciate your valuable feedback and I thank you for taking these copious amounts of food out of my kitchen.

Again, I could not have done this without the support of my family and friends. Thank you for helping me keep my priorities straight, and for lending a listening ear and for putting me in my place when I need it.

The team at St. Martin's Press continues to amaze and astonish me. I'm indebted to Michael Flamini for polishing the rough edges in the pages that come. And to Sarah and Nadea for all their help and hard work that it takes to get the $5 Dinners concept "out to the masses."

Thanks to my high school English teacher, Dr. Moss, for teaching me the basics of writing well. Writing has never been my forte. I much prefer the mathematical aspects of these $5 Dinners, quickly adding costs of ingredients as I go through the grocery store and figuring out how to tweak recipes so they can be made for less than $5. If you look closely enough, you will see her influence throughout these pages . . . and you will thank her too. She taught me how to structure paragraphs and papers with introductions and transitions. Her guidance is the reason that these cookbooks of mine flow and read as they do.

Lastly, I want to thank all the men in my life . . . big and little. I thank Steve for managing the dishes (although there weren't so many with the recipes in this book) with such a positive attitude, and for being an honest critic of dish after dish and meal after meal. And I thank Ryan, Charlie, and Tyler for being the best little taste test team in America. You all are my joy and my life and I couldn't imagine cooking and serving dinner every night for anyone else. I love you all.

The $5 Dinner Mom
One-Dish Dinners
Cookbook

INTRODUCTION

There was a time in my life when I could come home from work, sit down on the couch for a few minutes, check my personal e-mail, and then start to think about cooking dinner. I might not have had a plan, but I was just cooking for myself, or for my roommates, and soon after that for my husband and myself. We didn't spend a lot of money at the grocery store, we weren't pressed for time, and we didn't really have a need for meal planning at the time. We made what we felt like making with the simple ingredients that we had on hand.

Then we had kids.

And life changed for the better. Forever.

Life started costing more. And it started moving faster and faster . . . and faster. Exponentially so with each new addition to our family.

In an effort to combat the rising cost of everything from food to diapers to school snacks and lunches, I began a blogging Web site (www.5dollardinners .com) to share about the journey of making $5 Dinners for our family and spending less at the grocery store without sacrificing the quality of our meals. I wrote *The $5 Dinner Mom Cookbook* to get all the concepts, strategies, and recipes in one place so it would be an invaluable tool and resource that would help you reduce your grocery spending.

In an effort to help you streamline the rest of the day's meals and keep up with the ever-growing nutritional needs of your family, I wrote *The $5 Dinner Mom Breakfast and Lunch Cookbook*. It is filled with delicious and nutritious recipes and time-saving strategies for keeping the bottomless pits satisfied without spending all day, every day in the kitchen.

And now, in an effort to keep the dirty dishes in your sink to an all-time minimum and to help you keep up with life's time warp, I'm offering you *The $5 Dinner Mom One-Dish Dinners Cookbook*.

Before we get to the strategies and the recipes, let me present a quick history of the one-dish dinner, along with how I define it.

History of One-Dish Dinners

Do you know when and where the one-dish dinner concept originated? The concept started hundreds of years ago by people living out in the country who were poor and worked very hard day in and day out. Work was a matter of survival, not climbing career ladders or figuring out how much you need to save to retire. They worked hard to survive and to get food into their mouths. There was nothing convenient about living during these times. People needed to make simple meals that could be cooked in one pot using the few simple ingredients they raised in their fields, grew in their garden, or caught from the wild.

These pioneers had few options for cookware, possibly even limited to just one pot and one handmade knife, and maybe a wooden carving board. They may or may not have had an oven. And if they did, it wasn't the kind of oven where you could control or monitor the temperature. Baking bread one day might take an hour, and another day it might take two hours. Temperature control was a thing of the future. For these brothers and sisters of yester-centuries, skillet biscuits and cornbread made over the fire would have to do.

The One-Dish Dinner concept was born out of necessity. People needed to make simple meals with simple ingredients, using simple cookware. They needed to be able to eat dinner right out of the pot, while staying warm close to the fire.

Today, much of the world still cooks in these primitive-type settings. While living in the Dominican Republic, I saw lots of fire pits and makeshift outdoor stoves. Dominicans cook using their large Dutch oven–like pots, over a fire, and in large quantities to feed their family, their neighbors, and their neighbor's neighbors. Pigs are roasted on spits, and chickens are fried in the pots over a fire just outside the back door of the humble homes. The kitchens are not large with cabinet upon cabinet filled with stockpiles of food and an assortment of small kitchen appliances and cookware. It's an uncomplicated way of cooking.

Skillet dinners, casseroles and rice bakes, slow cooker meals, and grill dinners are newer additions to the One-Dish Dinners style of cooking, created to fit the lifestyle of the later 1900s and present day. And these kinds of modern-day dishes bring more options for minimalism into the kitchen and to the dinner table.

I have come to love One-Dish Dinners so dearly because of their ease and simplicity. Frankly, I still think I was born in the wrong era. I long for the days of old, and a one-dish dinner makes me feel like a pioneer. When I make one for my family, I can pretend that I'm cooking a simple dinner, over a small fire, on a plot of wide open land, filled with opportunity. I can satisfy my desire for simplicity in the kitchen, and bring the days of yesteryear back to the present by making healthy dinners for my family all in one dish.

Now, to define a One-Dish Dinner . . .

Definition of One-Dish Dinners

There are many people out there who are "one-pot purists," if you will. They believe that a one-dish dinner, or a one-pot meal, can only be cooked in a

Dutch oven and that's it. That's just a little too restrictive for this busy mom who would like a few more options and ways to get dinner on the table.

There are others who believe that the entire meal should be cooked in the same dish. The type of dish that the food is cooked in doesn't matter to this group, just as long as everything is in the dish. This concept is also still a little too restrictive for this mom who is trying to keep meals perfectly balanced for her family. While many, many one-dish dinners can be made this way, there are a few one-dish dinners that do best with a side of fresh fruit, or perhaps bread and butter.

For me, it's more about the preparation time and the number of dishes being used to make One-Dish Dinners. You will quickly see that most of the recipes call for just the dish they are cooked in. Some will also require a cutting board, while others will also call for a mixing bowl. *The fewer dishes, the better, right?!*

My husband, the resident dishmaster, certainly agrees!

During the recipe-testing phase, I was very conscious of the quantity of dishes used in making the different meals. In fact, on these "recipe-testing days," when I would make upwards of ten meals in one afternoon, Steve would come home and take one look at the sink and say, "How many recipes did you test today?"

I'd reply, "Only eight today."

To which he would respond, "That's it? This is all the dishes? Just half a sinkful?"

And I, too, would stand amazed at the amount of food that was prepared, compared to the number of dishes used to prepare it all.

For the dessert recipes, most only call for a mixing bowl plus the dish that the dessert is baked in. There is no need to get out three different mixing bowls, a hand mixer, a stand mixer, and eight different measuring cups and spoons. I'm all for minimal dishes, minimal time pulling dishware out of the cabinets, and minimal time at the sink cleaning up.

Every minute of prep time and every minute of cleanup time counts for this busy mom, who daily has to balance time in the kitchen with time building some new elaborate train-track scheme with her boys, watching them learn new tricks on their bikes or helping them learn how to read.

So I offer you a hybrid definition: *my one-dish dinner is a meal that is all cooked in the same dish with an occasional side dish accompaniment.*

The overall goals for my One-Dish Dinners are to make the preparation time shorter, to keep the dishes to a minimum, and to put balanced and healthful meals on the table for my guys. Every so often this requires the addition of bread and butter or fresh fruit, to complete the meal.

Also, I wanted to write a cookbook with recipes that do not require a cooking school degree, and that could be assembled easily by older children. I have also included recipes that will double easily for company, for the freezer, or for a friend or family member in need of a home-cooked meal. Other recipes are perfect for quick school-night suppers, make-ahead meals, or for when you just don't feel like spending more than 5 minutes in the kitchen.

The recipes that follow in this cookbook accomplish each of these goals and ideals.

About the Cookbook

Before we move on, here is a brief explanation of how the recipes in this cookbook are organized. Within each chapter, the recipes are ordered as follows: skillet dinners, casseroles, Dutch oven meals, slow cooker dinners, and dinners from the grill.

If you are looking for a quick recipe that uses chicken and you want to grill outside, then flip right to the end of the chicken and turkey chapter. If you are craving a vegetarian dinner and want to make it in the Dutch oven, then turn to the middle of chapter 10. I hope that the consistency in ordering the recipes helps you quickly find what you are looking for!

This cookbook contains 150 One-Dish Dinner recipes, complete with cost breakdowns and frugal facts. *Please note these recipes are written for a family of two adults and two children, but most recipes are portioned out to feed four adults.*

Larger families and/or families with teenagers will need to double or triple the recipes, depending on family size and the number of bottomless pits at the table.

The recipes call for common and inexpensive ingredients, like canned tomatoes, frozen spinach, pasta, beans, and other pantry and freezer staple ingredients (see Appendix A page 271). As you review and study the recipes, you will find that it's very much a "mix-and-match" game of combining these common ingredients in different ways, using different cooking methods to achieve different meal outcomes. And if you are familiar with the first two cookbooks and the prices included in them, you might notice that some of those prices have dropped in this cookbook. The most notable being a pound of pasta is now $.50, since I haven't paid more than that for a box of pasta in over a year. Also, I've cut the cost of olive oil in half because I have not paid more than $3 for a 17-ounce bottle in all of 2011. Other ingredient prices have dropped for the same reasons as these.

Also, I have included the phrases "Freezer Friendly," "Make-Ahead Meals," and "Slow Cooker Adaptable" on the appropriate recipes. Freezer Friendly indicates that the meal will freeze well *after it is cooked*. Make-Ahead Meals means that the recipe can be made in advance and frozen in a plastic freezer bags or a disposable aluminum-foil pan *before cooking*. And I have also indicated which recipes could also be cooked in the slow cooker. For the Slow Cooker Adaptable recipes, simply add all the ingredients listed on those marked recipes to the slow cooker and cook on low for 8 hours.

The prices associated with each ingredient are more or less standard throughout the book. Prices are accurate and reflect the best sale prices for the ingredients from late 2010 to middle of 2011. In the Midwest, I find that prices tend to be lower than other parts of the country, although if you watch the sales cycles closely, you can find the same sale prices in areas with a higher cost of living, such as northern California or the New York City area. Please do not expect to find these exact same prices in your stores. However, you should use the prices as benchmarks and to give you a sense of what prices you should be looking for when you are in the grocery store. I will teach you what to look for and how to find the rock-bottom prices on your favorite products from the grocery stores in your area.

The $5 Dinner Mom Recipe for One-Dish Dinners Success

1 cup shopping strategies

1 cup coupon strategies

2 cups meal-planning strategies

1 cooking vessel

1 cutting board or mixing bowl

1 pinch minimal fuss

Take 10 minutes to make the weekly meal plan, the grocery list, then spend 5 minutes putting together your One-Dish Dinners and letting themselves cook away.

Serve quick and easy One-Dish Dinner each night to hungry family.

The essence of my One-Dish Dinners—fewer minutes, fewer dollars, fewer dishes with full flavor and full nutrition.

Now that we've defined our recipe for One-Dish Dinners Success, let's get to the strategies that make One-Dish Dinners for less than $5 possible. I hope you catch on to the method to this madness, so that you, too, can feed your family wholesome, healthy, and balanced meals in a fraction of the time and at a fraction of the cost.

ONE

One-Dish Dinners Time- and Money-Saving Strategies

If the pioneers had only a few ingredients to work with and just a pot and a fire to make the simple one-pot meals they needed to survive, then we can too. Using simple ingredients and simple cooking methods, we can make meals that taste great and will give us the nutrition and fuel we need after a long day of work and play. The ease and convenience of cooking one-dish dinners will take you back to the days of old while bringing simplicity back to your next family meal, your next neighborhood block party, or church potluck.

In this first chapter, we will review the basic concepts of $5 Dinners and how they apply to my One-Dish Dinners. We will discuss the time- and money-saving strategies of today that will help you put a delicious and inexpensive one-dish dinner on the table that your family is sure to love.

Money-Saving Strategies

When it comes to making One-Dish Dinners for as little as possible, the same $5 Dinners rules, concepts, and principles apply. These recipes use common ingredients that can be found on sale every couple of weeks, and many of the ingredients can be purchased with a coupon during the sale for maximum savings. They also call for inexpensive cuts of meat and chicken. And, if there is an expensive ingredient, such as shrimp, the rest of the ingredients in the recipe are simple and inexpensive so that the overall cost of the meal stays under $5.

Let's review the strategies for shopping, couponing, and meal planning from *The $5 Dinner Mom Cookbook*, and how they can bring down the costs for your One-Dish Dinners.

STRATEGIC GROCERY SHOPPING

- Writing Your Grocery List Using the Store Circulars: Look at the store circulars *before* you go into the store and make your grocery list based on all the products listed on sale. Pay close attention to the sale prices for meats, chicken, and other expensive protein ingredients. Buy these products only when they are on sale and avoid paying double, or triple, in between sale cycles.

- Cash, Cash, Cash: Ditch the "plastic" and use cold hard cash at the checkout. This is crucial for staying within your budget. After all, you can't show up at the checkout with $100 worth of products and $75 in your hand. The store isn't going to trust you to come back in the next week with $25 you owe them.

- Defining Your Grocery Budget: Track your grocery spending for three months and come up with that magical dollar amount that works for your family. The number should be a challenge to reach each week, but still be a reasonable amount to get the ingredients you need each week.

- Avoiding Temptations and Spending Pits in the Grocery Store: Do not succumb to the marketing strategies that the stores and manufacturers use to get you to buy their products for top dollar or full retail. Remember: "I'll never pay full price again!"

- Never-Pay-More-Than Prices for Fresh Meats and Produce: In the Frugal Fact associated with each recipe, I'll share with you some examples of my "never-pay-more-than" prices for common ingredients used to make One-Dish Dinners.

STRATEGIC COUPONING

- Stockpiling and Rock-Bottom Prices: If you make it a habit to use coupons only when the product is on sale, then you'll be able to build a nice stockpile of foods for your pantry and freezer while spending as little money as possible. You can then make One-Dish Dinner after One-Dish Dinner using the ingredients from your pantry and freezer that you purchased at the lowest price possible.

• Coupon Organization: Remember that coupons are "free money" and that keeping them organized is essential to spending as little as possible on your favorite products each week. The 10 to 15 minutes per week time investment to keep your coupons in order is well worth the hundreds of dollars in potential savings each month.

STRATEGIC MEAL PLANNING

• Phases of Meal Planning: Take baby steps through the phases of meal planning. As a beginner, follow a "days-of-the-week" meal plan where you have pasta on Monday, slow cooker meal on Tuesday, pizza on Friday, etc. Once you get more comfortable trying new recipes with the ingredients you find on sale, start planning meals on a monthly basis with the food that you have in your stockpile and the meat that you have in your freezer. Eventually, you will decide whether to plan your meals and then shop, or shop from the store's circular and then plan your meals around what you have on hand.

• Stay Out of the Drive-Through Line: A meal plan each week will keep you out of the drive-through line and keep you from spending way too much money on an unplanned dinner out on the town.

• Leftovers: Having a plan for those dinner leftovers is essential, especially since many times lunch is when leftovers are eaten. With just one ingredient mix-in and some reheating, leftovers can easily be repurposed and enjoyed a second time.

• New Recipes—Make a goal of trying *three* new recipes each month. This will help keep your family from being bored with "the same old meal." These One-Dish Dinners recipes won't require any extra preparation time and will become like second nature after the first time making them.

One-Dish Dinners are both cost-efficient and time-efficient. After making just two or three of these recipes, you will quickly find that you are spending far less time in the kitchen preparing dinner than other non–One-Dish Dinner recipes.

Time-Saving Strategies

For the most part, One-Dish Dinners recipes are "dump and go," if you will. You dump it all into the pot, skillet, baking dish, or slow cooker and let it cook with an occasional stir. The cooking times do vary from 10 minutes to 1 hour plus, but the prep time is generally between 5 and 10 minutes for each recipe.

In the sections that follow, we will take some concepts from *The $5 Dinner Mom Breakfast and Lunch Cookbook* and twist them a bit to help you spend less time on the One-Dish Dinner prep. By putting the batch-cooking and precooked-ingredient concepts into practice, you could shave 20 to 30 minutes off of the preparation of some of the recipes in this cookbook.

BATCH COOKING

An essential to being prepared when it comes to One-Dish Dinners is the concept of batch cooking.

Batch cooking can be an hour that you set aside and devote only to preparing ingredients that you can freeze and use in One-Dish Dinners later in the month. It can be 10 minutes here and there when you prepare the food or chop vegetables while you are already making other meals in the kitchen. It can be when you plan to double the recipe for a favorite meal and stash the uneaten portion in the freezer for lunch the following week. It can be set up so you double every dinner that week so that you have several meals in the freezer to eat for the rest of the month. Or that you brown extra ground beef, or start a whole chicken in the slow cooker while you are already in the kitchen working on another meal.

The purpose of batch cooking is to maximize your time and efficiency in the kitchen, preparing and cooking your favorite foods from scratch, and without the burden of cooking for an entire day.

Precooked Ingredients

Another benefit of batch cooking is having precooked ingredients available from your batch-cooking efforts. Your batch-cooking efforts will cut down on meal prep time on a busy weeknight. If you already have ground beef browned, then you can have the Cheeseburger Potpie (page 141) ready to go into the oven before the oven has had time to preheat. Or you could have the Chicken, Tomato, and Herb Pasta Salad (page 71) chilling in the refrigerator before the kids ask for seconds of their afternoon snack, if you have some extra grilled chicken breasts in the freezer from last week's grill night.

- Batch Grilling Chicken Breasts: If you are grilling chicken breasts for dinner one night, why not grill a few extras to slice or dice and throw in the freezer. Then you'll have diced chicken ready for a quick pasta salad, or some sliced chicken to put on a salad or in a wrap. To thaw, set out the night before, or defrost in the microwave.

- Slow Cooker Whole Chickens: To cook a whole chicken in the slow cooker, simply add about 1 cup of water to the insert of the slow cooker, remove the giblets and neck from the cavity, and place the chicken in the slow cooker. If you wish to flavor the broth, add a few carrots and celery sticks. Season with garlic powder, onion powder, salt, and pepper. Set the slow cooker on low and cook for 8 to 10 hours. Once the chicken has cooked, carefully remove it from the slow cooker and place it on a serving platter or large tray. Let it cool for about 30 minutes before you pull the meat from the chicken and shred it. Let the meat cool and then place it into 2-cup portions in plastic freezer bags. Freeze the shredded chicken for up to 6 months. I suggest cooking the chicken overnight, letting it cool, and then pulling apart the chicken meat the next morning after breakfast or before you get lunch together. You can strain the stock from the slow cooker, let it cool, skim off the fat, and then freeze the stock to use in soups or stews. See Homemade Chicken Stock (page 256). Precooked and shredded chicken will allow you to prepare Chicken Succotash (page 90) or One-Dish Chicken Spaghetti (page 109) in a matter of minutes.

- Batch Cooking Dried Beans: Cooking with dried beans costs at least half as much as using canned beans. Generally I will plan a "batch-cooking morning" and include in the plan cooking a few different varieties of beans, then freezing them in 2-cup portions. This saves both time and energy, especially when it comes to cleanup. To cook the dried beans, soak them overnight in cold water, or for at least 2 hours in hot water. Then rinse the beans and place them into a large saucepan. Add water to the beans to cover them with about 2 inches of water. Bring to a boil, reduce the heat to low, and cook for about 1 hour to 1 hour and 15 minutes. Drain the beans in a colander and rinse with cool water. Let cool completely in the colander before placing them into the plastic bags to freeze. To thaw, place the sealed bags with the cooked and frozen beans in a bowl with hot water, or defrost them in the microwave.

- Browned Ground Beef: Purchase several extra packages of ground beef when you see it on sale for less than $1.49 per pound, or ground chuck for $1.79 per pound or less. In a large pot or Dutch oven, add 1 cup of water and then brown up to 5 pounds of ground beef at a time. Once browned, drain and let it cool before freezing it in 2- to 3-cup portions to use in different One-Dish Dinners, such as Beef and Zucchini Quesadilla Bake (page 137).

- Premade Meatballs: Another way to take advantage of the savings from a ground beef sale is to make meatballs, then freeze them before cooking. Then when you want to make Slow Cooker Spaghetti and

Meatballs Florentine (page 75), you can just drop them in with the sauce and move on with your day. If you purchase 10 pounds of ground beef on sale, brown 5 pounds and turn the other 5 pounds into several meals' worth of meatballs or 2 or 3 meat loaves. You already did the legwork perhaps while you were browning the rest of the ground beef you got on sale that day.

• Bacon and Sausage: Both of these ingredients can be batch cooked and the cooked slices or crumbles can be frozen to use for future meals. To quickly batch cook the bacon, place a piece of aluminum foil on a rimmed baking sheet and lay the bacon slices on the foil, with no overlapping. Bake at 350 degrees for about 20 minutes; the cooking time may vary depending on the thickness of the bacon pieces. Place the cooked bacon on paper towels to drain excess grease. Crumble or place whole slices into a plastic freezer bag or freezer container. Another "no-mess" way to cook bacon is to place 4 to 6 slices in between double layers of paper towels on a plate, and then microwave it for 3 to 5 minutes until it reaches the desired crispiness. Also, an entire roll of sausage can be crumbled and browned, or sausage links can be sliced, cooked, and then frozen. You can use the precooked bacon to quickly prepare the Loaded Potato Frittata (page 161), or the precooked sausage crumbles to make the Sweet-and-Spicy Sausage Cornbread Bake (page 159) in just minutes.

If you want to be able to have dinner prepared in 5 minutes or less, I suggest that you keep a steady supply of the following precooked ingredients in your freezer:

• Browned ground beef

• Meatballs, uncooked

• Cooked and shredded chicken

• Grilled chicken slices

- Diced grilled chicken

- Cooked beans of all varieties

- Cooked bacon

- Cooked sausage crumbles, slices, or links

Practical Look at Batch Cooking One-Dish Dinners

Okay, so how does batch cooking really work? What does it really look like? It's really a question of how well you can multitask and have several things cooking at once in the kitchen. It's about slow cooking dinner while baking a double batch of muffins and grilling chicken breasts to slice and dice, before freezing. Let's look at an example of how to batch cook ingredients for about nine meals in 1 hour (not including the slow cooker time).

- In the morning, place a whole chicken in the slow cooker with some vegetables to make shredded chicken and Homemade Chicken Stock (page 256).

- In the afternoon, brown 5 pounds of ground beef in a Dutch oven, drain, and let cool before freezing in 1-pound portions.

- Make 2 batches of meatballs (page 16) and freeze them raw.

- Brown 1 pound of ground sausage in a skillet to use for breakfast tacos, muffins, or breakfast scramble.

- Pull off the chicken meat from the slow-cooked whole chicken.

In an hour's time, you'll have pre-prepared the meat for nine different meals to enjoy that month.

During another hour of batch cooking, you could begin cooking 1 pound of three different varieties of dried beans, get several casseroles assembled for the freezer, and get a few packages of bacon cooked and into the freezer.

In the 5 minutes that it takes your kids to set the table, you can start a whole chicken in the slow cooker and cook it overnight. In the morning, you can pull off the shredded chicken, and strain the broth.

In the 20 minutes that it takes you to get spaghetti on the table, you can cook bacon in the oven. Then let it cool while you eat dinner and then drop the cooked bacon into plastic freezer bags while you clean up from dinner.

And in no extra grilling time at all, you could grill up 4 extra packages of chicken breasts or chicken thighs the week that you get them on sale. It will take you about 10 minutes to get the grilled and cooled chicken sliced or diced and packaged for the freezer.

To summarize these strategies, you have to be smart *before you go* into the grocery store by making your list using the store circular. You have to be smart *while inside* the grocery store by sticking to your list and paying with cash. You have to be smart with the *time that you spend* in the kitchen by batch cooking and precooking basic ingredients like ground beef and shredded chicken.

So you have both the time- and money-saving strategies all figured out, now let's move on to the mechanics, tips, and tricks of actually making the different kinds of One-Dish Dinners.

TWO

The Mechanics of One-Dish Dinners

As I made skillet dinner after skillet dinner and one Dutch oven meal after another, I learned a few practical and valuable lessons about the cooking methods and mechanics of One-Dish Dinners. Many of the cooking processes are similar in the different recipes and the different kinds of dinners. I hope that by providing you with a few basic guidelines for the different cooking processes, you will have the confidence it takes to get in the kitchen and start regularly making your family some delicious and inexpensive one-dish dinners.

In this chapter, we will go through the tips, tricks, and cooking processes for making skillet dinners, casseroles, and rice bakes, Dutch oven meals, slow cooker dinners and, finally, for making your entire dinner on the grill.

Skillet Dinners

Skillet dinners are for all you fast and furious moms, dads, grandparents, and caregivers, as they can be ready to go and on the table in 20 minutes or less, in most cases. The skillet dinners in this cookbook call for pasta, rice, or tortillas, some are of the "skillet-bake" variety, and there are a few "breakfast-for-dinner" frittatas. If making skillet dinners is new to you, I suggest reading through the following tips for each of the different kinds of meals to help you feel more comfortable in front of the stove.

PASTA

Pasta works wonderfully in a skillet dinner because it cooks quickly and does a good job absorbing the liquid from the skillet, which allows it to cook through evenly. The small pasta cuts, like small elbows, small shells, mini fusilli, or other piccolini pastas, all do really well in a skillet dinner because they can get into the smaller spaces in the skillet in between the other ingredients. Plus they cook faster, in 7 minutes or less, depending on the pasta cut.

When making a skillet dinner with pasta, it's important to remember the following things:

- Press the pasta down into the liquid in the skillet.

- Cover the skillet tightly and create a good seal so that you don't allow steam to escape and liquid to evaporate.

- Stir the pasta one time toward the beginning of the cooking time, and then quickly cover again so as little steam as possible escapes.

- Remove from the skillet from the heat as soon as the pasta is al dente. It will continue to cook a bit as it sits in the hot liquid. If you plan to make the dinner and let it sit for any longer than 15 minutes before dinnertime, I would transfer the cooked meal into a serving dish of some kind to avoid overcooking the pasta from the residual heat of the pan.

- When determining how much liquid is needed for the amount of pasta called for in the recipe, there is a basic ratio that I recommend. There are several factors that you need to consider when adding liquid to a pasta skillet dinner, including the type of pasta, how much liquid is already in the skillet from veggies sweating, how much liquid has already cooked off, and the size of the skillet or pot that's being used.

For quick-cooking pastas, regular pastas, and whole wheat pastas, you will need *2 cups of liquid for every 12 ounces of pasta* added to the recipe. Some of the liquid will already be in the skillet from the vegetables sweating or from items such as a can of tomatoes. The recipes recommend how much additional liquid you will need based on my experience from making them. But you will have to eyeball it and be sure there is enough liquid to cover most of the pasta. If you add too much liquid by accident, remove the lid of the pan and cook it off. And if you don't think you've added enough, just add some hot water, about ¼ cup at a time.

RICE

Many of these guidelines apply to cooking a rice skillet dinner, like the Stovetop Chicken, Broccoli, and Rice Casserole (page 106). The rice will overcook and get mushy if left in the skillet too long, or if not removed from the heat. Use a ratio of *2 cups liquid to 1 cup of white rice* when making rice skillet dinners. Also, I don't recommend using raw brown rice in a skillet dinner because it takes 45 to 50 minutes to cook, and the food at the bottom of the skillet will likely burn or close to it. If you prefer brown rice over white rice, then use a quick-cooking brown rice and follow the time guidelines listed on the package. You could also precook the brown rice in another pan or a rice cooker and freeze it in 2- or 3-cup portions. The frozen, cooked rice can be added to the skillet dinner along with ½ cup of hot water. Then just simmer long enough for the rice to warm up and integrate into the dish.

TORTILLAS

Several of the recipes call for torn tortillas to be added to a skillet dinner. Tortillas are extremely fragile in skillet dinners (and in soups, as well). They absorb liquid almost instantly, and will quickly turn to "tortilla mush." I recommend adding torn corn or flour tortillas just seconds before putting the skillet on the table for dinner. Or better yet, you could set out the tortilla pieces in a bowl and stir them into each serving bowl just before eating it.

SKILLET-BAKES

Some of our family's most favorite one-dish dinners are skillet bakes, like the Sloppy Joe Skillet Bake (page 128) and BBQ Chicken and Cornbread Skillet Bake (page 88). In a skillet bake, you sauté meat and veggies with a sauce, and then pour a batter or place bread on top of the meat sauce. Then, you bake the cooked contents in the skillet.

Before you make your first skillet bake, you should review the following:

- Skillet bakes generally cook best in a large 12-inch cast-iron skillet, but a deep, ovenproof 12-inch skillet or sauté pan will work as well.

- If the batter doesn't cover the contents of the sauce already cooking in the skillet, that's perfectly okay. It's fine if some of the juices from below bubble up around the cornbread or bread slices on top.

- Use heavy-duty oven mitts, as the skillet handle will be hot when it comes out of the oven. Leave the oven mitt draped over the skillet handle, or put the handle inside the oven mitt so that you will remember that it is still hot. You don't want to grab a piping hot skillet handle out of habit, forgetting it was just in a 350-degree oven. Ouch!

FRITTATAS

Frittatas are the breakfast for dinner, or what I call "brinner," skillet-bake options. My frittata recipes involve sautéing vegetables and some ham, bacon, or beef, and then pouring an egg mixture over the top. Then you let the eggs cook for a few minutes and "set" on the stovetop, before transferring the skillet to the oven. The frittatas are then baked for 15 to 20 minutes and are best served warm right out of the skillet. The same guidelines and principles of skillet bakes shared above apply. Just don't forget that the skillet handle will be hot, so use the oven mitt as described above and be sure to warn other family members that the handle is smoking hot so they don't get burned either.

You should now be fully equipped to make a skillet dinner or skillet-bake meal. So tomorrow night, get out the pasta and canned diced tomatoes from your pantry and some ground beef from the fridge or freezer and make the Skillet Lasagna Florentine (page 126) for your family.

Casserole Dinners

Casseroles are so warm and friendly. They ooze the feelings of home and, of course, often cheese. They are perfect for dinner, usually make great leftovers, and are perfect for gifts. They cook well, freeze well, and transport well, too.

You will find two types of casseroles in this cookbook. The first are traditional casseroles, like Beef and Zucchini Quesadilla Bake (page 137) and Bean Enchilada Casserole (page 220). And the second I call "rice bakes" if you will, such as Mango Chicken Curry Bake (page 104) and Spicy Orange Chicken Bake (page 100).

TRADITIONAL CASSEROLES

Casseroles are meals that are assembled easily, then generally baked for anywhere from 30 minutes to 1 hour. Some casseroles need to be covered, while others do not. You know a casserole is cooked when the meat inside has cooked through, the juices are bubbling, and the cheese on the top has melted and begun to turn golden. Mmmm.

RICE BAKES

A rice bake is a casserole that is made up of rice plus water, and other ingredients to make it a complete meal. It is then covered tightly with aluminum foil and the rice cooks as the casserole bakes. Most rice bakes using white rice take about 1 hour to cook in a 350-degree oven, or 1 hour and 15 minutes at 350 degrees when using brown rice. The rice cooks and steams in the water or other liquid in the dish, along with all the other flavors, and the final result is a tender, delicious rice bake.

Freezing Casseroles

When it comes to freezing casseroles, it's important to remember not to overbake them, as they will cook more when they are reheated. Also, be sure to cool them completely before freezing to reduce freezer burn. I prefer to "double wrap" my casseroles whenever possible. Smaller 8×8-inch or 9×9-inch disposable baking pans will fit snugly into a gallon-size plastic freezer bag. For larger 9×13-inch pans, I cover them tightly with aluminum foil and then wrap them with a layer or two of plastic wrap. This protects the food inside and keeps it from taking on any smells from other foods in the freezer. I also recommend keeping casseroles in the freezer compartment of the refrigerator no longer than 3 months, and in the deep freezer no longer than 6 months.

Casseroles can be frozen both before and after they are cooked. But for the most part, I recommend freezing them after they have cooked and cooled.

Below is a list of casserole ingredients that can be frozen, but don't freeze well:

- Onions lose flavor.

- Quick-cooking rice does not freeze well.

- Cooked potatoes lose texture after freezing.

- Bread crumbs are soggy after being frozen.

Now that we've mastered the art of freezing casseroles, we need to know the best methods for reheating them.

Reheating Casseroles

Many one-dish casseroles can be frozen both before and after they have been cooked. When it comes time to bake uncooked frozen casseroles, I recommend adding an additional hour to the baking time called for in the original recipe. So if an uncooked chicken casserole calls for an hour's baking time, I plan for at least 1 hour and 45 minutes to 2 hours if it is frozen. The frozen dish will need that extra time to defrost and then cook through in the oven.

With cooked casseroles that you wish to freeze, you'll be most successful if you cut them up into single-serve portions before freezing them. Each single portion can be wrapped in aluminum foil or plastic wrap, then frozen in a plastic freezer bag. Smaller portions reheat better, and having them cut into single-serve size will not only speed up the reheating time, but the defrosting time will be less as well. Single-serve portions can be defrosted in the microwave, and then quickly reheated in the microwave.

Another option is to place the entire cooked casserole that you want to reheat in the refrigerator for a day or two before cooking, giving it time to defrost slowly. Once defrosted, the casserole can be warmed at 350 degrees for 30 minutes.

If you wish to cook a frozen casserole that was made with raw meat ingredients, then defrost completely before baking in the oven as directed in the recipe, and until the meat is cooked through.

Casseroles on the Go

So you've got a casserole that's been in the freezer waiting for a friend or family member who needs a delicious home-cooked meal. What's the best way to get it there? Well, you have two transport options: frozen or cooked.

Let's say that you have it all defrosted and reheated or cooked, but now it's time to get it to your friend or family member in one piece without making a mess all over your car. First, use an insulated casserole dish carrier and add a small thermos filled with warm water to keep it hot. If you don't have an insulated carrier or cooler, then wrap the warm casserole in towels or newspaper to keep it insulated while you transport it to your friend's house, your church, or your aunt across town. I highly suggest placing the casserole dish in a box as well. Because even if it is tightly covered with foil or a baking dish cover, the contents can still leak out the sides with a sudden stop or bend in the road.

Frozen casseroles are easier to transport because they are solid. However, if a frozen casserole will be out of the freezer for longer than 30 minutes while you transport it, I recommend using a cooler or cooling pack to keep it cold and frozen while you transport it.

Quick-and-Easy Casserole Cleanup

If you are busy in the kitchen making several meals at once and really need to keep cleanup to a minimum, I recommend the following options:

- Aluminum Foil–Lined Casseroles: Casserole and baking dishes can be lined with foil for easy cleanup. So save yourself some elbow grease and some dish soap by lining the baking dish with foil. Also, foil-lined casseroles can be easily frozen and once frozen, the baking dish underneath removed and freed up for another use.

- Disposable Baking Dish: If you are doubling a recipe, consider cooking the second portion in a disposable baking dish. Then you can easily put the disposable dish in the freezer that you can use later for a meal of your own, or to save for a friend of family member who is in need of a meal. You can also make the second portion in a foil-lined baking dish, and then freeze the portion in the dish. Once frozen, you can remove the frozen food, wrap foil around it, label it, and return it to the freezer. This way your baking dish is not trapped in the freezer with the second portion of last night's dinner.

Next stop, Dutch oven One-Dish Dinners!

Dutch Oven Dinners

Dutch oven dinners are soothing, filling, and best made with inexpensive meats. They are flexible, as you can braise, sear, stew, slow cook, or bake with them. Perhaps their flexibility is why they worked so well in the pioneer days. Pioneer cooks also used them to fry or scramble eggs, cook bacon over the fire, and more.

Nowadays, many people use their Dutch ovens for outdoor cooking over a campfire. The traditional Dutch oven was made with feet. This makes me wonder if the pioneers had the luxury of a pot with feet, or if they just had to balance it carefully on hot rocks or straight on the coals.

When it comes to cooking meat in a Dutch oven, the slower and longer you cook it, the more tender the meat will become. High heat and short cooking time will result in tough meat and a not so tasty dinner. However, in some recipes, you will want to use high heat to initially brown or sear the meat or chicken. And after that, reduce the heat and cook the food for a minimum of 30 minutes. Dutch ovens also do a wonderful job of simmering chilis, soups, and stews for long periods of time, allowing their flavors to mix and mingle in the pot.

Speaking of stews, if you want a thicker base in your Dutch oven soups or stews, whisk in a teaspoon of cornstarch at a time, allowing it a few minutes to cook into the liquid and thicken. If you need more, add one more teaspoon at a time until it reaches the desired consistency.

When adding cheese to a Dutch oven dinner, I suggest adding it about 5 minutes before you are ready to serve the meal. Sprinkle shredded cheese over the top, reduce the heat to low, and allow the cheese to melt over the top. Once the meal is cooked and cheese has melted, remove the Dutch oven from the burner and serve immediately.

When serving Dutch oven dinners, like chilies or stews that call for a side of bread and butter, consider placing the bread slice in the bottom of each serving bowl and allowing it to soak all the delicious juices. This works best using thick slices of sourdough bread or French bread.

When serving a warm Dutch oven dinner on a cold winter night, I suggest warming the chili, soup, or stew bowls by running them under hot water and patting them dry. You could also place ovenproof serving bowls in a warm oven, set for 200 degrees for 10 minutes before you plan to serve the dinner.

Leftover chilis can be repurposed into tacos and burritos. They are also tasty when added into the center of a pie crust pouch. Cut Homemade Pie Crust (page 267) into 4-inch circles and then wrap them around a ½ cup of chili, making a "chili tart." Bake at 350 degrees for 10 to 15 minutes until the crust is cooked through and the chili is warm.

FREEZING DUTCH OVEN DINNERS

When freezing cooked Dutch oven dinners, be sure to let them cool completely before adding them to the plastic container that you will freeze them in. This will reduce the potential for freezer burn. First, place the container in the refrigerator and let the food cool completely; then transfer to the freezer. You also want to leave at least ½- to 1-inch of headspace at the top of the plastic container, as the food will expand as it freezes.

It's important to note that cornstarch does not freeze well, so if you make a stew or chili that calls for cornstarch, you'll need to eat it all up or reheat the leftovers for lunch the next day.

REHEATING DUTCH OVEN DINNERS

Dutch oven dinners can be stored in the refrigerator while still in the pot they were cooked in. Just be sure that you cool them down and then place a trivet into the refrigerator if the bottom is still warm. To reheat, simply place the entire pot over low heat on the stovetop and let simmer for 20 to 30 minutes until warm. If you wish to reheat a single portion, just scoop out what you need and warm it in the microwave.

DUTCH OVEN DINNERS ON THE GO

Dutch oven dinners can be taken on the road with a little care and protection of the carpet in your car. They should be wrapped with towels, or newspaper, and secured with rubber bands, to prevent the lid from slipping off. Also, I suggest placing them into a box for transport, to keep any spills from staining your car's interior.

Many of the Dutch oven recipes found in this cookbook could also be made in the slow cooker. Both use the same low-heat, slow-cook concept in the preparation of the food. Dutch ovens work well for those who like to cook on a regular basis, or if you forget to start the slow cooker that morning. Slow cookers work wonders for those who don't have much time for anything other than "dump and run."

Slow Cooker Dinners

My absolute favorite part of slow cooker meals is that you barely have to lift a finger and you've got dinner on the table. Many slow cooker meals can be put together in less than 5 minutes. Others take a few more minutes to prep vegetables and gather ingredients for a sauce. Others require a little attention towards the end of the cooking cycle, such as for adding pasta or rice. But compared to the hands-on time required for a similar recipe made the "traditional way," the time commitment is a fraction of what it could be.

Slow cooker meals are perfect for when you need a simple way to make home-cooked comfort food. It's wonderful to come home from a long day of work, or a busy afternoon of errands, to a house filled with the delicious smells of your favorite stew or roast. You can't help but thank the slow cooker for working so hard for you all day, as you pass through the kitchen on your way to change into your around-the-house clothes.

Slow cookers generally cook on a low setting and a high setting, for either preset periods of time, or programmable amounts of time. Some slow cookers can be programmed to start at a certain time of day, which is perfect for the busy working family. Simply check the owner's manual of your slow cooker, or do your research to understand the different slow cooker options before purchasing one.

Slow cookers work by cooking the food at lower temperatures (compared to the oven or stovetop) for longer periods of time. This allows the meats cooked in the slow cooker to turn out more tender than if they had been cooked using another method. Slow cookers also work as self-basters, as when the steam produced by the cooking food reaches the underside of the lid, it falls back down over the food.

A few important things to remember when making slow cooker meals:

- Do not open the lid to stir the contents. Slow cookers lose heat quickly when the lid is opened. The bubbling created by the slow heat will naturally stir the contents in the slow cooker.

- Read the recipe carefully, as some recipes call for the slow cooker to be partially covered (although no recipes in this cookbook call for that).

- Slow cookers work best when they are at least half full.

RICE AND PASTA

Many slow cooker recipes call for the addition of rice and pasta at the end of the cooking cycle. If you were to add the rice and pasta at the beginning of the cooking cycle, you would end up with a pile of mush because the long cooking process would overcook the rice and pasta. It's best to add rice and pasta toward the end of the cooking cycle (see times below). Also, if you don't plan to serve the meal with rice or pasta from the slow cooker right away, then transfer the cooked meal into another serving bowl. The warm setting and the warm stoneware slow cooker insert will continue to cook the rice and pasta, turning it into a mushy mess.

Use these times as a guideline for when to add pasta and rice to the slow cooker:

- Brown rice: 2½ hours left in the cooking cycle when on high, 3 hours when on low.

- White rice: 2 hours left in the cooking cycle when on high, 2½ hours when on low.

- Wild rice: 3 hours left in the cooking cycle when on high, 3½ hours when on low.

- Medium shell pasta: 25 to 30 minutes before the end of the cooking cycle when on high or low.

- Small shell, or other quick-cooking pasta: 18 to 20 minutes before the end of the cooking cycle when on high or low.

- Whole grain pasta: 35 to 40 minutes before the end of the cooking cycle when on high or low.

Because adding frozen vegetables to a slow cooker meal can add extra liquid, it's best to defrost them before adding them to the slow cooker. Place them in a colander in the sink and run water over them until they defrost, then add the veggies to the slow cooker as called for in the recipe.

MAKE-AHEAD MEALS

When you plan a batch-cooking day, you should add make-ahead slow cooker meals to your list. To prepare make-ahead meals for your slow cooker, simply add all the ingredients called for in the recipe (with the exception of pastas or rice) into a large gallon-size plastic freezer bag. Include the cut-up veggies, meat, and sauce/dressing/marinade in the bag. Add a short label to the baggie that includes the recipe name and how long you are to cook it in the slow cooker, along with any additional ingredients and instructions beyond "dump and go."

Freeze the meal and then write it onto your freezer inventory list or onto your monthly meal plan. You don't want to forget that you've already prepared the meal and put it in the freezer. To use, I recommend defrosting it overnight and then adding it to the slow cooker and cooking for the appropriate amount of time. If the contents are still partially frozen, consider adding an additional 2 hours of cook time.

A perfect make-ahead slow cooker meal is the Balsamic Pot Roast with Pearl Onions (page 153). Add the chuck roast and the balsamic vinegar, Italian seasoning, and salt and pepper first. Then toss in the potato chunks, carrot pieces, and the frozen pearl onions. Label and freeze.

Other simple make ahead slow cooker meals are Slow Cooker Pork Roast with Sweet Potatoes and Apples (page 174), Pot Roast with Dilled Carrots and Potatoes (page 148) and Chipotle Chicken Tacos (page 117).

SLOW COOKER CLEANUP

Slow cookers can be tough on the elbow grease, especially if you use a tomato-based sauce like BBQ sauce in the slow cooker. These tomato-based sauces tend to harden and sometimes burn around the edge of the slow cooker, making them tough to clean out.

There are, however, a few things that you can do to make the cleanup process even faster. You can add additional liquid to the slow cooker before you cook the food, but no more than 1 cup's worth. The extra liquid will create a moist environment inside the slow cooker and help prevent the food or sauce from sticking to the edges.

Also, you can line it with the plastic slow cooker liners that are sold in most grocery stores. While this would cost a little bit more to purchase the liners, it might be worth it for when you are using your slow cooker(s) for preparing food for a party and you need the cleanup to be as simple as possible after the party. Because, really, who wants to scrub out a slow cooker after hosting a fun night with friends or family?! I think it's wise to have a box of slow cooker liners in the drawer along with your foil and plastic wrap, and then use them sparingly.

SLOW COOKER ON THE GO

When taking the slow cooker on the go to a potluck, friend's house, or church event, I suggest protecting it in two ways. You don't want the contents to be spilling out all over your car. I recommend either wrapping the entire slow cooker in towels, to help with both insulation and spillage. If you only have a short distance and aren't concerned about the potential heat loss, then place 2 or 3 large and heavy-duty rubber bands around the base to secure the lid. And finally, I'd place any slow cooker in a large box before putting it in the car. This will make it easy to carry, you won't burn your hands or need oven mitts, and it will keep any spillage from getting into the car's carpet.

OUTDOOR COOKING

Another important thing to remember about the slow cooker is that you can put it out in your garage or on your back porch to cook your food. This is perfect for those hot summer months when every fraction of a degree matters in the house and in the kitchen. You can make your favorite shredded BBQ pork sandwiches in the slow cooker without heating up your kitchen. Also, putting your slow cooker outside works perfectly for pregnant moms, who just can't stomach the smell of cooking food, but still need to feed their families. Just be sure that the slow cooker is protected from any threat from outdoor critters, who might be tempted by the delicious smells.

Using your slow cooker outside and making dinners on the grill is the perfect combination for some summertime "outdoor batch cooking." Let's move on to dinner on the grill, shall we?

Dinner on the Grill

When it is just too hot to think about turning on the oven, or even cooking something on the stovetop, it's time to take your cooking energies out to the back patio. The grill is not just for burgers, brats, hot dogs, and chicken. It can be used to cook vegetables, potatoes, and even bread. That being said, an entire dinner made on the grill is totally a reality.

The best one-dish dinners on the grill are grill packets and kebabs served with a side of grilled garlic bread, and of course, grilled pizza.

Grill packets are made up of a meat of some sort, along with some vegetables and flavorings, wrapped in a foil pouch and then cooked on the grill. To make grill packets ahead of time, simply place all the ingredients into the grill packets and wrap the foil tightly around the contents. Place the foil packets flat into a plastic freezer bag and lay them flat in the freezer, to keep any olive oil or sauce from spilling out. Let thaw completely before cooking on the grill. Another advantage to make-ahead grill packets is that the meat or chicken will marinate as it thaws. Add some garlic bread (page 268) to the grill while the packets are cooking and you've got a complete dinner from the grill.

Kebabs and garlic bread are another simple and easy "one-grill dinner." Any variety of kebab, chicken, beef, pork, or veggie will work. Add a dipping sauce, like ranch dressing or pizza sauce, to round out the meal.

Another important aspect of grilling meats and chicken is marinating and brining. Marinating is a method in which you "soak" the meat in a sauce or oil-based dressing. It's best to marinate foods for at least 30 minutes, but the longer the better. If you are grilling or roasting a larger cut of meat, such as a whole chicken, you can inject marinade deep into the meat to allow the flavors to penetrate throughout.

Brining helps tenderize different meats before you grill them. If you brine chicken, meat, or pork chops before grilling them, they will have a soft, tender, and delicious texture when cooked. To brine a meat, simply place it in a baking dish and submerge it in heavily salted water. Brine for at least 2 hours and no more than 24. After brining, I recommend rinsing the meat and patting it dry before grilling, to keep the salty flavor from taking away from the tender, juicy outcome.

Grilled pizzas are smoky-licious. Our family adores grilled pizza, and if you haven't tried it, I highly recommend starting with the Grilled Pizza Pockets (page 81). Pile the meat and vegetables on top of the crust with some sauce and cheese and grill it up. Thicker, fuller Homemade Whole Wheat Pizza Dough (page 263) works better on the grill than uncooked store-bought pizza crusts. They tend to be too soft, have a tendency to fall through the grill grates, and are unable to hold the weight of the toppings. If you do want to try using an uncooked store-bought pizza crust, lay it flat on a baking sheet and place it in the freezer for about 20 minutes to allow the crust to harden up. Then when you place it on the grill, it will still cook up fast enough, but not droop through the grill grates.

THE GRILL'S HEAT TYPES

When grilling, you need to understand the two different types of heat that your grill produces. A grill can generate both direct heat and indirect heat, depending on the size and shape and the location of the heat source.

- Direct heat is directly over the heat source, and should be used for searing meats, such as chicken beef, or pork, to seal in their juices. But use caution, because if you cook meat too long over high direct heat, your food can burn, dry out, and become too tough to eat.

- Indirect heat can be found in the parts of the grill that are not directly above the heat source. It could be a section of the grill where the heat source directly below is not turned on, or it could be on the upper rack on the grill. Indirect heat is best for cooking meats for longer periods of time. The best place to cook hot dogs or marshmallows is over the indirect heat.

For most meat, I recommend cooking it over direct heat for a few minutes on each side, then transferring it to a different location over indirect heat to finish the cooking. Your meat will turn out perfectly smoky-licious and with those perfect "grill marks."

With your skillet dinners cooked to perfection, your slow cooker meals mastered, and your "one-grill dinners" cooked to smoky-licious perfection, let's chat for a second about serving one-dish dinners.

Serving One-Dish Dinners

Just like the pioneers did back in the old days, one-dish dinners can be served right out of the pot. Casseroles can be placed in the middle of the table, Dutch ovens can be kept warm over low heat on the stovetop and served buffet style, and you can dish out bowls of soups or stews straight from the slow cooker— a few examples of the simplicity, ease, and convenience of one-dish dinners. And if you need to add a quick side dish of fresh sliced fruit, some bread and butter, or a small side salad alongside your one-dish meal, you will still have a simple dinner to serve and easy cleanup.

I hope that you feel three-hundred times more confident in trying to make some of the One-Dish Dinners featured in the following chapters, having learned about the cooking processes and some of the important techniques and suggestions for making the perfect dinner in one-dish.

THREE

One-Dish Dinners Cookware

But before we move on to the recipes, we need to do a quick overview of the common cookware used in making one-dish dinners. While I may long for the pioneer days of the past, it is wonderful to live in an age where we have so many options available to use for making dinner. It can also be overwhelming and difficult to decide on the best brand of Dutch oven, the best size of slow cooker, or best kind of grill.

In this chapter, I will share with you the kinds of cookware that I used for testing the recipes, along with how to best care for the cookware and the best places and prices for purchasing the different pieces.

About the Cookware

SKILLETS

To make a skillet dinner that will serve four people, you will need to use a large nonstick skillet, at least 12 inches in diameter and 1 to 1½ inches deep, or a 5-quart sauté pan that has deep sides. There's nothing worse than starting on a meal, only to realize that your pan is not large enough to contain the contents of your recipe. (Ask me how I know!) That completely defeats one of the main purposes of making one-dish dinners, doesn't it?!

A cast-iron skillet does a wonderful job of retaining heat and distributing it to the food inside. It does take a while to warm up and get hot, but once warm, it does a wonderful job of cooking a wide variety of foods. A cast-iron skillet also releases iron into your food. It can be used for sautéing vegetables, baking a cake, and frying potatoes. Cast-iron skillets are long lasting, and in some families they are passed down from generation to generation. I used a 12-inch preseasoned cast-iron skillet when testing the cast-iron skillet recipes. I seasoned it twice during the recipe testing phase of writing this cookbook.

CASSEROLE DISHES

My casseroles are typically baked in rectangular glass baking dishes. The glass does a wonderful job of evenly distributing the heat to the ingredients in the dish. The glass makes reheating in the microwave or oven simple. And being able to transfer the casserole dish straight from the oven to a trivet on the dinner table makes the getting to the dinner table much smoother.

Casseroles can also be made in disposable aluminum foil pans for easy freezing and transport. If you prefer to use oval casseroles or gratin dishes over rectangular baking dishes, then use the following recommendations for proper sizes:

- 3-quart oval dish = 9 × 13-inch baking dish

- 2-quart oval dish = 7 × 11-inch baking dish

- 1½ quart oval dish = 8 × 8-inch baking dish

When making the casserole and rice-bake meals included in the cookbook, I used the rectangular or square glass baking dishes specified in each recipe.

DUTCH OVENS

Dutch ovens come in a variety of sizes and are generally round in shape. For large family meals, you will want to use a 5-quart or larger Dutch oven. Dutch ovens are quite versatile, as you can cook anything from bacon to soups to cornbread inside of them. They can do everything that skillets, baking dishes, and sauté pans can do. And if you had to choose just one type of cookware to take with you to a deserted island, I would suggest you take a Dutch oven. Most Dutch ovens also come with a self-basting lid, meaning the underneath side of the lid is designed to encourage the steam droplets to fall back down into the soup or over the chicken or beef that is cooking inside.

If you don't have a Dutch oven, then don't sweat. The recipes in this cookbook that call for cooking in a Dutch oven can also be cooked in a large heavy-bottomed pot.

For the Dutch oven and pot recipes in this cookbook, I used a 5-quart cast-iron enameled Dutch oven with a self-basting lid or a stainless steel 6-quart Dutch oven/pot with a lid.

SLOW COOKER

When an entire meal is to be cooked with a slow cooker, I recommend using an oval-shaped 5-quart or larger ceramic slow cooker with both high and low settings, and one which has the most control over the time settings. Slow cookers do an amazing job of cooking the less expensive cuts of meat like pork shoulder roast and beef chuck roasts. They make the most tender roast, and make perfect shredded chicken, too. The smaller, circular 2-quart slow cookers with just the high and low setting work better used for dips and fondues.

I used the 6-quart Crock-Pot brand Elume slow cooker when making all the slow cooker recipes in this cookbook.

GRILL

When it comes to selecting a grill, the two options are gas and charcoal. With both, there will be the additional cost of charcoal or propane gas from a tank or line from your house. And when it comes down to it, it's just a matter of personal preference as to which to choose. Some people love the ease of the gas grill, while other folks have to have the added smoky flavor from cooking over charcoal. You can utilize both the direct and indirect methods of grilling (page 38) with both the gas and charcoal grills.

For the grill recipes, I used a Weber gas grill that has an upper deck grill rack that is perfect for indirect heat grilling.

Now that we have established the different sizes and shapes of the required cookware pieces, let's chat for a minute about how to take care of it all so that your investment is worthwhile.

Caring for One-Dish Dinners Cookware

There's no sense investing in quality cookware if you don't know how to take care for it and make it last a lifetime. The following tips and tricks for cleaning and storing your One-Dish Dinners cookware will help it last and last.

SKILLETS

I recommend cleaning your skillets with soap and hot water. Stainless steel skillets can withstand the dishwasher, but I suggest running them through the dishwasher only 2 or 3 times a month.

If the bottom of your skillet is encrusted with food after cooking, you will want to deglaze it while it is still very hot by pouring hot water into it to help the crust loosen from the skillet. Then rinse the skillet out and scrub out any remaining food. Soaking the skillet with hot water and dish soap overnight will also make it easier to wash by hand.

Many cast-iron skillets come preseasoned, but they lose their seasoning over time. I suggest that you season your cast-iron skillet (and other cast-iron cookware) every couple of months, depending on how often you use it. To season a cast-iron skillet, simply coat the inner surfaces with cooking oil and place it in a 350-degree oven for an hour. Then let it cool and dry it well with paper towels and it will be ready to use.

Cast-iron skillets clean best immediately after you finish cooking with it. Rinse it with warm water, and if there is a stubborn spot of burned food, gently rub it with some kosher salt and a plastic scrub brush or scrub pad to try to release it.

Cast-iron skillets also need to be dried completely before storing. Failure to do so will result in a rusty cast-iron skillet. Designate a special kitchen towel that you only use for drying your cast-iron cookware, as they often will smudge the towel.

CASSEROLES

Food can stick easily to glass and metal casserole dishes, mostly because of the way the food cooks around the edges of the dish, and because the leftovers often sit in the refrigerator for several days after the casserole was made. Casserole dishes clean best after soaking overnight in warm water with a few drops of dish soap. Both glass and metal casserole dishes can be washed in the dishwasher. And another tidbit about taking care of your glass baking dishes—do *not* add cold water to a hot baking dish in the oven. It will shatter. And make a terrible, shardy mess in your oven.

DUTCH OVENS

Stainless steel Dutch ovens or pots should be washed immediately after cooking, and they are safe to put in the dishwasher. Because they have a greater risk of forming a crust on the bottom when cooking, it's best to rinse them while still hot, and soak with warm water and dish soap. Then scrub them out by hand and wash in the dishwasher every now and again.

Enameled and cast-iron Dutch ovens should never go in the dishwasher. Both respond best to being rinsed with hot water as soon as you are finished cooking or serving dinner, using a plastic scrub pad or stiff plastic scrub brush. You should never use dish soap or a metal scrub brush or scrub pad on a cast-iron skillet or Dutch oven that is not enameled.

SLOW COOKER

The stoneware or ceramic insert in most slow cookers needs to be handled and cleaned with care. The stoneware can be cleaned with hot, soapy water. Whatever you do, do not add cold water to a hot slow cooker. The dramatic change in temperature can cause cracks in the stoneware. Most slow cooker lids are dishwasher-safe, but I do not recommend washing the stoneware insert in the dishwasher. To clean the inside and outside of the heating base use a cloth and warm soapy water once the heating base has completely cooled.

GRILL

I recommend that you clean the grill gates every time you use the grill. The best way to keep the grill grates clean is to turn on the grill, close the hood, and let it warm up to 300 degrees or so. Then run the wire scraper up and down along the grates, scraping off all the leftover food particles. Then let the grill finish warming up and place your dinner on to cook. You can also scrape the food particles from the grill grates immediately after cooking your food and while the grill is still hot. The hot grill makes it easier to remove the food particles from the grill grates.

Be sure to check your owner's manual to make sure you don't have to do anything special for cast-iron or enameled grill grates.

Keep cleanup of charcoal grills simple by lining the bottom of the grill with heavy-duty foil. Let the coals and grill cool completely before throwing the foil and used charcoal into a nearby trash can.

Also, it's important to give your grill a thorough cleaning at the end of each grilling season. The following needs to happen before you store your grill for the winter:

- Turn off gas supply and disconnect it all from the tank or house line.

- Remove the grill grates and flame guards.

- Clean out the soot and grease from the interior.

- Replace the disposable grease tray. Or clean the permanent grease tray with hot water and soap.

- Scrub the grill's grates.

- Clean out the gas lines.

- Put the grill back together once all parts are completely dry.

- Clean the outside of the grill with soap and water, or stainless steel cleaner if it is a stainless steel grill.

- Reconnect gas supply when ready to use again. Cover for the cold season.

Replace the grill grates and flame guards when they show signs of rust or chipping. You want to be sure to follow these cleaning guidelines to keep your grill, your "fourth kitchen appliance," in top working condition, so that it lasts for years and years. You want to get your money's worth from this investment. And, maintaining a clean grill keeps food tasting the way it should taste.

Now onto how much the different kinds of cookware should cost. It's time to find out how much money should be invested in good quality One-Dish Dinners cookware.

Cost of One-Dish Dinners Cookware

Skillets and sauté pans can be found at home-goods stores, online retailers, and even some high-end grocery stores. They range in price from $20 to $250 depending on the brand and material used in making the skillet. I'd recommend spending somewhere in the middle range, as you will use the skillet week in and week out, year-round. You can use it to scramble eggs, cook sausage, brown ground beef, and make complete skillet dinners. It's a very versatile cooking tool.

Cast-iron skillets, just like skillets and sauté pans, can be purchased from home-goods retailers, online retailers, and most grocery stores. A good-quality preseasoned 12-inch cast-iron skillet can cost as little as $20.

Casserole dishes can be purchased in most places, from the grocery store to major home-goods retailers. Also, I often see glass baking dishes at garage sales and in thrift stores for $1 and less. This is a great way to add to your collection without having to pay full price. The normal retail price for casseroles dishes ranges from $6 to $20 depending on the size and shape. I would recommend getting a set that contains a lid, which is helpful for storing casseroles in the refrigerator and for transporting them to a picnic, potluck, or friend's house.

A good-quality Dutch oven can be purchased for anywhere from $50 to

$250. I don't believe that it is necessary to invest $250 in an expensive name-brand Dutch oven. Spending $45 to $50 on a cast-iron Dutch oven will be the better investment in the long run. I bought my Dutch oven at Cost Plus World Market when it was on sale. That store also releases regular $10 off $50 purchase-type coupons, so you could get one very inexpensively.

Slow cookers range widely in price for the 5- and 6-quart sizes. They can be found new for as little as $25, and upwards of $200. Most major home-goods retailers carry slow cookers. Be sure to look online, or sign up for e-mails from the store to find out about specials and get coupons for shopping in their store, or for certain products. Just as with grocery shopping, look for the best deal—when the product is on sale and you have a coupon to use as well!

As I said, the grill is really the fourth major kitchen appliance after the stove, dishwasher, and refrigerator. And by thinking about a grill in this way, you will understand that it's important to research the different options, and even pay a little bit more for quality when selecting one. It will be well worth the investment. I spend several nights a week for four to five months out of the year standing in front of the grill, or watching my husband flip burgers or kebabs. That being said, I need and want to have a good-quality grill to cook your summertime dinners.

Gas grills can range anywhere from $150 to $2000 depending on their size and grilling capabilities. Portable gas grills that sit on a tabletop can be found for as little as $60. Charcoal grills can be purchased for between $30 and $300 depending on their size and height.

Important grill accessories to have on hand include a long-handled spatula, long-handled tongs, and a charcoal starter, if you have a charcoal grill, and a grill grate cleaning tool with mesh and wire scrub pads. These tools retail for around $5 to $7 each. Also, having a mesh grill basket or grill skillet ($5 to $20) is essential for making Chicken and Potatoes Grill-Fry (page 123).

Of course, keep an eye out for these cookware pieces that are gently used and still in good condition when you are visiting online resale Web sites such as www.craigslist.org, thrift stores, garage sales, or consignment shops. You never know when you will happen upon an amazing cookware deal!

So we have laid out the money and time-saving aspects of One-Dish Dinners, we discussed the important points to know about the cooking processes for the different recipes included in the cookbook, and we went over a few guidelines to follow when actually making the meals. We've also checked out the different options and what to look for in the stores when purchasing cookware, the specific sizes of cookware, and how to care for your cookware.

I'd say it's time to move on to the tasty part of the cookbook—the 150 simple, inexpensive, wholesome, and delicious One-Dish Dinners recipes that follow!

Ham and Broccoli Breakfast "Brinner," *page 173*

Red Quinoa with Avocado, Black Beans, and Corn, *page 230*

Braised Chicken with Radishes, Carrots, and Red Potatoes, *page 110*

Beef Stew Biscuit Bake, *page 149*

Southwest Mac and Cheese, *page 63*

Mango Chicken with Roasted Zucchini, *page 94*

Pizza Penne Bake, *page 60*

Mango-Raspberry Crumble, *page 238*

FOUR

Pasta, Pizza, and Sandwich One-Dish Dinners

Cajun Macaroni and Cheese Skillet

1 pound ground beef ($1.49)
1 cup frozen chopped green bell
    pepper ($.40)
1 cup frozen chopped onion ($.40)
½ cup chopped celery ($.10)
2 tablespoons Creole seasoning ($.25)
1 can (15 ounces) diced tomatoes,
    with their juices ($.20)

1 cup milk ($.10)
1½ cups hot water
2 cups elbow macaroni ($.25)
¼ cup sour cream ($.25)
1 cup shredded cheddar cheese ($.63)

Fresh fruit, such as orange wedges or apple slices ($.50)

In a large 12-inch skillet or sauté pan over high heat, brown the ground beef. Drain and return it to the skillet.

Add the bell peppers, onions, and celery with the Creole seasoning. Sauté for 4 to 5 minutes until the pepper and onion have thawed and the onions are translucent. Stir in the diced tomatoes.

Add the milk and hot water. Stir in the elbow macaroni and press into the liquid. Cover and let cook for 8 to 10 minutes. Uncover once halfway through the cooking time, and stir the macaroni to make sure it doesn't stick to the bottom of the skillet.

When the pasta is al dente, remove the skillet from the heat and stir in the sour cream and the shredded cheese. Let cool slightly before serving.

Serve Cajun Macaroni and Cheese Skillet with fresh fruit.

Makes 4 servings

Cost $4.57

FRUGAL FACT: *Transform your favorite comfort food with this recipe, simply by adding some Creole seasoning and the trio of classic Cajun cooking: onions, green bell peppers, and celery.*

Creamy Linguini with Asparagus and Peas

....

8 tablespoons butter ($.80)

2 garlic cloves, crushed ($.05)

¼ cup all-purpose flour ($.05)

4 cups milk ($.40)

1 pound asparagus, trimmed and
cut into 1-inch pieces ($.99)

1 bag (12 ounces) frozen peas ($.80)

8 ounces linguini, broken ($.25)

¼ cup hot water

In a large 12-inch skillet or sauté pan, melt the butter over medium heat. Add the garlic and sauté for 1 minute. Whisk in the flour and then slowly pour in the milk, whisking constantly. Cook for at least 1 minute. Reduce the heat to medium-low and continue to cook, whisking often until the sauce begins to thicken and bubble.

Once the sauce is bubbling, add the asparagus and frozen peas. When the peas have thawed, stir in the broken linguini and the hot water. Cover tightly and simmer for 9 to 11 minutes. Uncover once halfway through the cooking time, and stir the linguini to make sure it doesn't stick to the bottom of the skillet.

When the linguini is al dente, remove the skillet from the heat. Let cool slightly before serving.

Serve Creamy Linguini with Asparagus and Peas.

Makes 4 servings

Cost $3.34

FRUGAL FACT: *If you prefer to make this with chicken, either top it with some batch-grilled and sliced chicken (see page 14), or add cubed batch-grilled chicken to the prepared sauce. You can still keep this meal just slightly over $5.*

Skillet Black Bean Lasagna

3 cups cooked black beans ($.60)

1 can (15 ounces) diced tomatoes, with their juices ($.20)

1 can (15 ounces) corn kernels, drained ($.50)

1 can (4 ounces) green chilies, with their liquid ($.79)

1 teaspoon ground cumin ($.05)

1 teaspoon chili powder ($.05)

Salt and pepper

6 lasagna noodles, broken into 1-inch pieces ($.45)

2 cups hot water

2 cups shredded Mexican blend cheese ($1.25)

Sour cream, for serving ($.10)

In a large 12-inch skillet or sauté pan, combine the beans with the diced tomatoes, corn, and the green chilies. (If you prefer, you can substitute two 15-ounce cans rinsed and drained black beans for the 3 cups of cooked black beans.) Mix in the cumin, chili powder, and salt and pepper to taste. Bring to a boil over medium-high heat and add the broken lasagna noodles and hot water. Gently stir the mixture in the skillet and press the lasagna pieces into the liquid. Reduce the heat to medium, cover, and cook for 15 to 20 minutes, stirring once.

When the pasta is al dente, uncover the mixture and top with the shredded cheese. Cook for another 2 to 3 minutes over low heat to allow the cheese to melt.

Serve Skillet Black Bean Lasagna warm.

Makes 4 servings

Cost $3.99 (Note: The cost will change with the substitution of canned beans.)

FRUGAL FACT: *Stock up on canned beans when they go on sale for less than $.70 per 15-ounce can.*

Lasagna Your Kids Will Love!

9 lasagna noodles ($.75)

¾ pound ground beef, browned ($1.12)

1 can (15 ounces) crushed tomatoes, drained ($.20)

1 box (10 ounces) frozen chopped spinach ($.50)

1 tablespoon dried Italian seasoning ($.15)

½ teaspoon garlic powder ($.03)

Salt and pepper

¼ cup grated Parmesan cheese ($.25)

2 cups cottage cheese ($1)

1 ¼ cup shredded mozzarella cheese ($.79)

Preheat the oven to 350 degrees. Grease an 8 × 8-inch glass baking dish with nonstick cooking spray.

Cook the spinach in the microwave as directed on the package. Drain well.

In a large pot or Dutch oven, boil the lasagna noodles as directed on the package. Drain and lay out on a clean kitchen towel.

In a mixing bowl, combine the ground beef, crushed tomatoes, cooked spinach, Italian seasoning, garlic powder, and a little salt and pepper to taste.

Place the lasagna noodles in the bottom of the prepared baking dish, cut off the excess length, and save the pieces for the middle layer. Spoon half of the meat mixture over the lasagna, then sprinkle with half of the grated Parmesan cheese and spread 1 cup of the cottage cheese on top. Repeat the layering, using the cut excess lasagna noodles for the middle layer, the remaining meat mixture, Parmesan cheese, and cottage cheese. Top with the remaining lasagna noodles and the shredded mozzarella cheese.

Bake in the preheated oven for 25 to 30 minutes until bubbly and the cheese is beginning to turn golden. Let cool slightly before cutting and serving.

Serve Lasagna Your Kids Will Love!

Makes 4 servings

Cost $4.79

FRUGAL FACT: *Get the kids to eat vegetables by including them in their favorite lasagna dinner.*

FREEZER FRIENDLY

Pizza Penne Bake

1 pound medium tubular pasta, such as penne or ziti ($.50)

¾ cup store-bought or Homemade Pizza Sauce (page 259) ($.31)

1 red bell pepper, seeded and chopped ($1)

1 green bell pepper, seeded and chopped ($.59)

About 30 slices pepperoni, cut in half ($1)

¼ cup grated Parmesan cheese ($.25)

1 cup pizza blend shredded cheese ($.63)

Salt and pepper

Preheat the oven to 350 degrees.

In a large Dutch oven or ovenproof pot, cook the pasta as directed on the package. Reserve ¼ cup of the pasta water and then drain the pasta.

To the same Dutch oven or pot, add the reserved pasta water and the pizza sauce and whisk together. Stir in the bell peppers and pepperoni slices. Cook for 2 to 3 minutes, then add the drained pasta and toss to combine with the sauce. Season with salt and pepper to taste.

Sprinkle the Parmesan cheese over the pasta and then sprinkle the pizza blend shredded cheese over the top. Place the Dutch oven or ovenproof pot into the preheated oven and bake for about 10 minutes, or until the cheese melts.

Serve Pizza Penne Bake warm.

Makes 4 servings

Cost $4.28

FRUGAL FACT: *Make this simple one-dish pasta when you've got a craving for pizza but you don't have the time to make up a homemade pizza crust and you don't have a store-bought crust on hand.*

FREEZER FRIENDLY

One-Dish Spaghetti Dinner

....

1 pound ground beef ($1.49)

1 small yellow onion, chopped ($.20)

2 garlic cloves, crushed ($.05)

1 can (15 ounces) tomato sauce ($.20)

1 can (15 ounces) diced tomatoes,
  with their juices ($.20)

1 tablespoon sugar ($.01)

2 teaspoons dried Italian
  seasoning ($.10)

4 carrots, peeled and grated ($.40)

Salt and pepper

3½ cups store-bought or Homemade
  Beef Broth (page 257) or water
  (free, if homemade)

1 pound thin spaghetti, broken into
  thirds ($.50)

Side salad with Homemade Basic Vinaigrette (page 261) ($1.50)

In a large pot or Dutch oven over medium high heat, brown the ground beef with the onion and garlic. Drain and return the mixture to the pot.

Add the tomato sauce, diced tomatoes, sugar, Italian seasoning, and carrots. Season with salt and pepper to taste. Simmer the sauce over medium-low heat for 5 to 10 minutes.

Increase the heat to medium and add the broth or water. Stir in the broken thin spaghetti pieces and press into the sauce so they are submerged in the liquid. Cover the pot and let cook for 7 to 9 minutes.

When the spaghetti is al dente, remove the pot from the heat. Let cool slightly before serving.

Serve One-Dish Spaghetti Dinner with a small side salad.

Makes 4 servings

Cost $4.65 (Note: The cost will change with the substitution of store-bought beef broth.)

FRUGAL FACT: *Why dirty an extra pot to cook the spaghetti, when you can cook it in the pot along with the sauce?*

FREEZER FRIENDLY

Southwest Mac and Cheese

1 pound elbow macaroni ($.50)

1 cup sour cream ($1)

1 can (10 ounces) diced tomatoes with green chilies, with their juices ($.50)

2 cups cooked black beans ($.40)

1 can (15 ounces) corn kernels ($.50)

2 cups Mexican blend cheese, or Pepper Jack cheese blend, divided ($1.25)

In a large pot or Dutch oven, cook the macaroni as directed on the package. Drain and set aside while you prepare the sauce.

In the same pot, combine the sour cream, diced tomatoes with green chilies, beans, and corn. (If you prefer, you can substitute one 15-ounce can rinsed and drained black beans for the 2 cups of cooked black beans.) Add the drained macaroni to the mixture and stir in about 1½ cups of the shredded cheese.

Serve Southwest Mac and Cheese warm from the pot. Sprinkle the remaining cheese on top of each serving.

Makes 4 servings

Cost $4.15 (Note: The cost will change with the substitution of canned beans.)

FRUGAL FACT: *Freeze shredded cheese when you find it on sale for $1.25, or even less if you have the right coupon matchup.*

Easy Pea-sy Macaroni Salad

1 pound elbow macaroni ($.50)

2 carrots, peeled and chopped ($.20)

2 green bell peppers, seeded and
  diced ($1.18)

1 small red onion, chopped ($.40)

1 bag (12 ounce) frozen peas,
  cooked ($.80)

DRESSING

½ cup light mayonnaise ($.25)

3 tablespoons lemon juice ($.15)

3 tablespoons vinegar ($.15)

4 tablespoons sugar ($.04)

Salt and pepper

Fresh fruit, such as cantaloupe wedges or bananas ($.50)

In a large pot or Dutch oven, cook the elbow macaroni as directed on the package. Drain and return it to the pot, or transfer it to a serving bowl.

Toss the carrots, bell peppers, onion, and peas with the pasta.

In a small mixing bowl, whisk together the mayonnaise, lemon juice, vinegar, sugar, and salt and pepper to taste. Pour the dressing over the pasta and toss well. Chill the salad in the refrigerator for at least 2 hours before serving.

Serve Easy Pea-sy Macaroni Salad with fresh fruit.

Makes 4 servings

Cost $4.17

FRUGAL FACT: *In a time crunch and don't have time for the salad to chill in the refrigerator for 2 hours?! Simply run cold water over the pasta for 2 to 3 minutes after it drains and reduce the overall chilling time to 10 to 15 minutes.*

Bow-Tie Pasta with Bacon, Corn, and Parmesan

12 ounces bow-tie pasta ($.50)

1 can (15 ounces) diced tomatoes with basil, garlic, and oregano ($.20)

6 bacon strips, cooked and crumbled ($.75)

1 can (15 ounces) corn kernels ($.50)

⅓ cup grated Parmesan cheese ($.33)

1 teaspoon garlic powder ($.05)

1 teaspoon onion powder ($.05)

Salt and pepper

Side salad with Homemade Basic Vinaigrette (page 261) ($1.50)

In a large pot or Dutch oven, cook the pasta as directed on the package. Drain and return it to the pot, or transfer it to a serving bowl.

Add the diced tomatoes, bacon, corn, cheese, garlic powder, and onion powder to the pasta and toss to combine. Season with salt and pepper to taste.

Serve Bow-Tie Pasta with Bacon, Corn, and Parmesan with a side salad.

Makes 4 servings

Cost $3.88

FRUGAL FACT: *If you batch cook the bacon and have it ready and waiting in the freezer, you can have this dinner on the table in less than 20 minutes. If you don't have the bacon cooked ahead of time, you can microwave it between double layers of paper towels (page 17) while the pasta is cooking, and still have dinner on the table in 20 minutes.*

Italian Pasta Salad

....

12 ounces rotini pasta ($.37)

40 slices pepperoni, cut into
  quarters ($1.25)

1 green bell pepper, seeded and diced
  into ¼-inch pieces ($.59)

1 block (4 ounces) cheddar cheese,
  cut into ⅛-inch cubes ($.67)

⅓ cup green olives, chopped ($.50)

1 teaspoon Italian seasoning ($.05)

½ cup store-bought or Homemade
  Basic Vinaigrette (page 261) ($.25)

In a large pot or Dutch oven, cook the pasta as directed on the package. Drain and rinse with cool water, then return to the pot or transfer to a large serving bowl.

Toss the pepperoni slices, the bell pepper, cheese cubes, and olives with the pasta, add the Italian seasoning, and then stir in the vinaigrette dressing. If you wish to serve the salad cold, chill it in the refrigerator for at least 2 hours.

Serve Italian Pasta Salad, chilled or at room temperature.

Makes 4 servings

Cost $3.68

FRUGAL FACT: *Purchase whole block cheese and then cut off the portion that you need for the pasta salad, saving the rest to use with crackers or thinly sliced for sandwiches. It can be up to 50 percent less expensive than buying the pre-cut cheese cubes in bags.*

Lemony Pasta with Ham and Peas

....

1 pound penne pasta ($.50)

1 bag (12 ounces) frozen peas ($.80)

2 cups cooked cubed ham ($2)

DRESSING

¼ cup extra-virgin olive oil ($.20)

½ teaspoon lemon zest

Juice of 1 lemon ($.25)

½ teaspoon dried dill ($.05)

Salt and pepper

¼ cup grated Parmesan cheese ($.25)

In a large pot or Dutch oven, cook the pasta as directed on the package. Drain and return it to the pot, or transfer it to a serving bowl.

Steam the peas in the microwave, according to the package directions. Toss the peas with the pasta and cooked ham.

In a small mixing bowl, whisk together the olive oil and lemon juice. Stir in the lemon zest and dill, and season with salt and pepper to taste. Pour the dressing over the pasta, peas, and ham, then sprinkle the cheese over the top. Toss well. If you wish to serve the salad cold, chill it in the refrigerator for at least 2 hours.

Serve Lemony Pasta with Ham and Peas, warm or chilled.

Makes 4 servings

Cost $4.05

FRUGAL FACT: *With a good coupon matchup, frozen vegetables can often be bought for as little as $.50 per 12-ounce package. With the perfect coupon matchup, they can even occasionally be bought for free.*

Angel Hair Pasta with Grilled Chicken and Julienned Zucchini

....

12 ounces angel hair pasta ($.37)

1 tablespoon extra-virgin olive oil ($.05)

1 small zucchini, about ⅔ pound, julienned ($.50)

2 garlic cloves, crushed ($.05)

1 teaspoon dried Italian seasoning ($.05)

Salt and pepper

2 cups diced grilled chicken ($1.50)

½ cup grated or shredded Parmesan cheese ($.50)

In a large pot or Dutch oven, cook the pasta as directed on the package. Drain and set aside.

In the same pot, heat the olive oil, add the zucchini, garlic, and Italian seasoning and sauté for 4 to 6 minutes until the zucchini is tender. Season with salt and pepper to taste.

Add the drained, cooked pasta and chicken. Add the cheese and toss with the pasta, chicken, and vegetables.

Serve Angel Hair Pasta with Grilled Chicken and Julienned Zucchini.

Makes 4 servings

Cost $3.02

FRUGAL FACT: *If you have basil, oregano, and parsley growing in your garden, use fresh herbs for a more fragrant flavor.*

Creamy Herbed Pasta Salad

12 ounces ziti pasta ($.37)
1 green bell pepper, seeded and
  chopped ($.59)
1 cucumber, seeded and
  chopped ($.50)

1 plum tomato, seeded and
  diced ($.50)
4 eggs, hard boiled, peeled,
  and chopped ($.40)

DRESSING

½ cup light mayonnaise ($.25)
¼ cup milk ($.03)
2 teaspoons lemon juice ($.04)
1 teaspoon parsley ($.05)
1 teaspoon basil ($.05)

1 teaspoon garlic powder ($.05)
1 teaspoon minced onion ($.05)
½ teaspoon dried dill ($.05)
Salt and pepper

Fresh fruit ($.50)

In a large pot or Dutch oven, cook the pasta as directed on the package. Drain and rinse with cool water and return it to the pot, or transfer it to a serving bowl.

Add the bell pepper, cucumber, tomato, and hard-boiled eggs and toss to combine with the pasta.

In a small mixing bowl, whisk together the mayonnaise and milk with the lemon juice, parsley, dill, basil, garlic powder, and onion. Add the dressing to the pasta and vegetables and toss well to combine. Season with salt and pepper to taste.

Chill the salad in the refrigerator for at least 30 minutes.

Serve Creamy Herbed Pasta Salad with fresh fruit.

Makes 4 servings

Cost $3.43

FRUGAL FACT: *Save yourself a mess on the cutting board or in a mixing bowl, and carefully cut the hard-boiled eggs with the prongs of a fork in the palm of your hand over the pasta. Press the fork prongs down on the egg and flat against your hand, as to not injure yourself. Once the egg pieces are small enough, let the cut pieces of the egg fall into the bowl with the pasta.*

Chicken, Tomato, and Herb Pasta Salad

12 ounces rotini or medium shell pasta ($.37)

2 cups diced grilled chicken ($1.50)

2 plum tomatoes, seeded and diced ($1)

DRESSING

¼ cup extra-virgin olive oil ($.40)

⅛ cup white wine vinegar ($.10)

⅛ cup lemon juice ($.10)

2 tablespoons chopped fresh herbs, such as basil, oregano, dill, and rosemary ($.25)

½ teaspoon garlic powder ($.03)

Salt and pepper

In a large pot or Dutch oven, cook the pasta as directed on the package. Drain and return it to the pot, or transfer it to a serving bowl.

Add the diced chicken and tomatoes and toss with the pasta.

In a small mixing bowl, whisk together the olive oil, vinegar, lemon juice, fresh herbs, garlic powder, and salt and pepper to taste. Pour the dressing over the pasta, chicken, and tomatoes and toss to combine. If you wish to serve the salad cold, chill in the refrigerator for at least 2 hours.

Serve Chicken, Tomato, and Herb Pasta Salad, warm or chilled.

Makes 4 servings

Cost $3.75

FRUGAL FACT: *To quickly chop fresh herbs, roll up the smaller herbs inside of a basil leaf to resemble a cigar, then chop the fresh herbs. This will help keep smaller* *herb leaves within the group of herbs and guarantee they are cut and their aromatics released into your meal.*

Vegetable Garden Pasta Salad
with Feta Cheese

....

1 pound penne pasta ($.50)

1 red bell pepper, seeded and
diced ($1)

1 yellow bell pepper, seeded and
diced ($1)

1 cucumber, diced ($.50)

4 ounces feta cheese, crumbled ($1.50)

½ cup store-bought or Homemade
Basic Vinaigrette (page 261) ($.25)

Salt and pepper

In a large pot, cook the penne pasta as directed on the package. Drain and rinse with cold water.

While the pasta is cooking, toss the bell peppers, cucumber, and feta cheese crumbles together in a serving bowl. Add the drained, cooled pasta and the vinaigrette and toss to combine. Season with salt and pepper to taste.

Chill the salad in the refrigerator for at least 2 hours before serving.

Serve Vegetable Garden Pasta Salad with Feta Cheese.

Makes 4 servings

Cost $4.75

FRUGAL FACT: *There's no need to heat up the kitchen on a hot summer night when you can make this perfect, light summer pasta with vegetables from the garden or from the local farmers' market. Prepare this delicious dinner in the morning and let it chill all afternoon.*

Farm Stand Mac and Cheese

1 pound elbow macaroni ($.50)

2 small broccoli heads, cut into florets ($.79)

1 tablespoon extra-virgin olive oil ($.05)

1 small zucchini, about ⅔ pound chopped ($.50)

2 garlic cloves, crushed ($.05)

1 cup milk ($.10)

½ cup sour cream ($.50)

2 cups shredded sharp cheddar cheese ($1.25)

1 can (15 ounces) sweet peas, drained ($.50)

In a large pot or Dutch oven, cook the macaroni as directed on the package. During the last 5 minutes of cooking, add the broccoli florets to the cooking pasta. When the pasta is al dente and the broccoli turns bright green, drain and set aside while you sauté the zucchini.

In the same pot or Dutch oven, heat the olive oil. Add the zucchini and sauté for 3 to 5 minutes until the zucchini is tender. Stir in the milk and heat until bubbling. Add the cooked pasta and broccoli and quickly stir in the sour cream and shredded cheese. Stir constantly for 1 to 2 minutes until the cheese has melted and the pasta is creamy.

Stir in the sweet peas.

Serve Farm Stand Macaroni and Cheese warm.

Makes 4 servings

Cost $4.24

FRUGAL FACT: *My "never-pay-more-than" price for a 1-pound box of pasta, excluding lasagna or manicotti, is $.50. It can often be purchased for less than $.25 per pound, and occasionally for free with the right coupon matchup.*

Slow Cooker Spaghetti and Meatballs Florentine

1 pound ground chuck ($1.79)
2 eggs ($.20)
1 tablespoon minced onion ($.10)
1 teaspoon dried Italian
   seasoning ($.05)
1 box (10 ounces) frozen chopped
   spinach ($.50)

1 can (28 ounces) crushed
   tomatoes ($0.59)
½ teaspoon garlic powder ($.03)
Salt and pepper
8 ounces spaghetti, broken into
   thirds ($.25)
½ cup hot water

In a mixing bowl, mix together the ground beef, eggs, onion, and Italian seasoning. Form the mixture into 16 to 20 small meatballs.

Cook the frozen spinach in the microwave as directed on the package. Drain well.

Place the meatballs into the insert of a 5-quart or larger slow cooker. Pour the crushed tomatoes, the cooked and drained spinach, and the garlic powder over the top. Gently stir to combine the tomatoes, the spinach and garlic powder.

Set the slow cooker on low and cook for 8 hours. When there are 30 minutes remaining in the cooking cycle, add the broken spaghetti and the hot water and complete the cooking cycle. Remove the spaghetti and meatballs immediately from the slow cooker stoneware insert. Leaving the pasta in the slow cooker, even on the warm setting, will cause it to overcook and turn it to mush. Season with salt and pepper before serving.

Serve Slow Cooker Spaghetti and Meatballs Florentine.

Makes 4 servings

Cost $3.51

FRUGAL FACT: *If you forget to add the broken spaghetti and the cooking cycle switches to warm, just add the pasta and water and let cook for about 45 minutes on the warm setting.*

Dutch Oven Biscuit Pizza

½ pound ground Italian sausage ($1)

15 slices pepperoni, halved ($.50)

¾ cup store-bought or Homemade Pizza Sauce (page 259) ($.31)

1 cup frozen chopped onion ($.40)

1 cup frozen chopped green bell pepper ($.40)

1 cup shredded mozzarella cheese ($.67)

BISCUIT TOPPING

1¾ cups all-purpose flour ($.35)

¼ cup yellow cornmeal ($.08)

1 tablespoon sugar ($.01)

1 tablespoon baking powder ($.15)

1 teaspoon dried Italian seasoning ($.05)

½ teaspoon garlic powder ($.03)

4 tablespoons butter, melted ($.40)

1 cup milk ($.10)

Preheat the oven to 350 degrees.

In a Dutch oven or a large ovenproof pot, brown the ground Italian sausage. Drain and return it to the pot.

Stir in the pepperoni slices, pizza sauce, onion, and bell pepper. Cook over medium-low heat for 5 to 7 minutes.

In a mixing bowl, whisk together the flour, cornmeal, sugar, baking powder, Italian seasoning, and garlic powder. Whisk in the melted butter and milk.

When the batter is ready, sprinkle the cheese over the bubbling sausage mixture and then pour the biscuit batter over the top. Transfer the Dutch oven to the preheated oven and bake for 20 to 24 minutes until the biscuit crust is baked through and beginning to turn golden on top.

Using heavy-duty oven mitts, carefully remove the Dutch oven pot from the oven. Let cool slightly before serving.

Serve Dutch Oven Biscuit Pizza warm.

Makes 4 servings

Cost $4.45

FRUGAL FACT: *If you are looking to clear out your pantry and you have canned black olives and/or canned sliced mushrooms, drain them and add them to the sausage mixture for a "supreme biscuit pizza" that will cost you just over $5—still much cheaper than a pizza delivery!*

FREEZER FRIENDLY

Grilled Chicken Caesar Flatbread

2 pieces flatbread, about 10 inches each ($1.49)

½ cup store-bought Caesar salad dressing ($.33)

2 boneless, skinless chicken breasts, grilled and sliced ($1.88)

2 cups romaine lettuce, finely chopped ($.50)

½ cup shredded Parmesan cheese ($.50)

Cracked black pepper

Salt

Grease the grill grates with nonstick cooking spray. Preheat the grill for indirect cooking on low heat.

Place the flatbreads on the grill grates and spread the Caesar salad dressing over the flatbreads. Add the chicken, lettuce, and cheese on top. Sprinkle with some cracked pepper and a little salt as well.

Cover the grill hood and grill the flatbread for 5 to 7 minutes until warmed through.

Serve Grilled Chicken Caesar Flatbread.

Makes 4 servings

Cost $4.70

FRUGAL FACT: *If you can't find flatbread in your grocery store, roll out 4 small thin, thin-crust pizza crusts using the Homemade Whole Wheat Pizza Dough recipe (page 263). The thin crust will cook in 5 to 7 minutes on the grill.*

Grilled Veggie Pizza

1 bag (12 ounces) California-style
   frozen vegetable blend ($.88)
1 can (8 ounce) tomato sauce ($.33)
1 teaspoon dried Italian
   seasoning ($.05)

1 recipe Homemade Whole Wheat
   Pizza Dough (page 263) ($.97)
2 cups shredded cheddar or
   Colby-Jack cheese ($1.25)

Preheat the grill for indirect cooking on low heat.

Cook and drain the frozen vegetables, as directed on the package.

Open the can of tomato sauce and gently stir in the Italian seasoning.

Roll out the pizza crust dough on a clean, lightly floured surface. Place the crust on a large, lightly floured cutting board or baking sheet. Spread the herbed tomato sauce over the entire crust, add the cooked vegetables on top, and sprinkle with the shredded cheese. Carefully slide the pizza onto the grill.

Grill the pizza over low heat for 10 to 12 minutes, or until the crust has cooked through and cheese has melted.

Serve Grilled Veggie Pizza.

Makes 4 servings

Cost $3.48

FRUGAL FACT: *Cut the prep time in half by using a prebaked store-bought crust and placing it on the grill. If you use an uncooked pizza crust, roll it out and place it in the freezer for 30 minutes before placing it on the grill; this will prevent the crust from falling through the grill grates.*

Grilled Pizza Pockets

1 recipe Homemade Whole Wheat
    Pizza Dough (page 263) ($.97)
1 can (8 ounces) tomato sauce ($.33)
1 teaspoon dried Italian
    seasoning ($.05)
24 slices pepperoni ($.75)

1 cup frozen chopped green bell
    pepper ($.40)
1 cup frozen chopped onion ($.40)
2 cups shredded mozzarella
    cheese ($1.25)

Preheat the grill for indirect cooking on low heat.

Open the can of tomato sauce and gently stir in the Italian seasoning.

Roll out the pizza crust dough and divide it into 8 small dough balls. Roll the small dough balls out on a clean and lightly floured surface into an oval shape. Add a dollop of herbed tomato sauce to each of the pieces of rolled out dough, then top with the pepperoni, bell pepper, and onion. Divide the shredded cheese evenly among the 8 pieces of dough and sprinkle over each. Fold the dough over and pinch the edges together. Carefully transfer the pizza pockets to the grill.

Grill the pizza pockets for 5 to 6 minutes on each side until the crusts have cooked through and cheese has melted.

Serve Grilled Pizza Pockets, hot off the grill.

Makes 4 servings

Cost $4.15

FRUGAL FACT: *You can use whatever favorite pizza toppings you have on hand for these grilled pizza pockets—sliced mushrooms, browned sausage crumbles, or ham and pineapple.*

Mexican Pizza Bites

6 English muffins ($.99)
1 cup store-bought salsa or Homemade
  Salsa Fresca (page 260) ($.75)
1 cup cooked black beans ($.20)
½ cup sliced black olives ($.50)
1 cup frozen chopped green bell
  pepper ($.40)

1 plum tomato, seeded and
  chopped ($.50)
3 sprigs fresh cilantro, chopped ($.25)
1½ cups shredded Mexican blend
  cheese ($.96)

Preheat the oven to 350 degrees.

Split the English muffins in half and lay them open faced on a baking sheet. Spread a dollop or two of salsa on each of the English muffins.

In a small mixing bowl, combine the beans, olives, bell pepper, tomato, and cilantro. Add a spoonful of the mixture to each of the English muffins. Top with a pinch of the shredded cheese.

Bake the muffins in the preheated oven for 10 to 12 minutes until the cheese has melted. Let cool slightly before serving.

Serve Mexican Pizza Bites.

Makes 4 servings

Cost $4.55 (Note: The cost will change with the substitution of canned beans and/or store-bought salsa.)

FRUGAL FACT: *During the late winter and early spring, stock up on the inexpensive pre-chopped frozen vegetables, like chopped bell pepper, chopped onion, and stir-fry vegetables. Being able to grab a cup of chopped bell pepper from the freezer will dramatically reduce your prep time.*

FREEZER FRIENDLY

Kid's Krazy Pizza Faces

6 English muffins ($.99)
½ cup store-bought or Homemade
   Pizza Sauce (page 259) ($.21)
24 slices pepperoni ($.75)
1½ cups shredded pizza blend
   cheese ($1)

1 red bell pepper, cut into 12 thin
   strips ($.75)
12 black olive slices ($.05)
2 baby carrot sticks, cut into rounds
   ($.05)

Baby carrot sticks ($.50)

Preheat oven to 350 degrees.

Split the English muffins in half and lay them open faced on a baking sheet. Spread a dollop or two of pizza sauce on each of the English muffins. Lay 2 pepperoni slices on each English muffin and then top with a pinch of shredded cheese.

Make faces with the bell pepper strips as the mouth, the sliced olives as the nose, and the carrot rounds as eyes.

Bake the mini pizzas in the preheated oven for 10 to 12 minutes until the cheese has melted. Let cool slightly before serving to hungry children.

Serve Kid's Krazy Pizza Faces with baby carrots.

Makes 12 mini kid pizzas

Cost $4.30

FRUGAL FACT: *Purchase a few extra bags of English muffins when they are on sale or a Manager's Special and freeze them. Then let the kids help you fix this fun (and quick) lunch on the weekend.*

Grilled Turkey, Swiss, and Mushroom Panini

1 white onion, sliced ($.20)

8 ounces sliced white button mushrooms ($.99)

8 slices whole grain bread ($1)

1 tablespoon Dijon or spicy mustard ($.05)

6 ounces sliced turkey ($1.50)

4 slices Swiss cheese ($.75)

Fresh fruit, such as orange wedges or slices or apple slices ($.50)

Prepare a grill for indirect cooking over medium heat.

Place the sliced onions and sliced mushrooms in a grill basket or skillet and grill or sauté for 5 to 10 minutes until they begin to brown. If you don't have a grill basket or a grill, then sauté them in a skillet on the stovetop until they begin to brown.

Spread the mustard on the bread slices, and once the onions and mushrooms are cooked, begin the sandwich assembly. The assembly order is as follows: 1 bread slice, ½ slice Swiss cheese, 1 slice turkey meat, pinch of grilled onions and mushrooms, ½ slice Swiss cheese, and the remaining bread slice.

Place the sandwich on the grill and press down with an aluminum foil–covered brick or other heavy object. Grill for 4 to 5 minutes on each side until the cheese has melted and bread has brown grill marks.

Serve Grilled Turkey, Swiss, and Mushroom Panini with fresh fruit.

Makes 4 paninis

Cost $4.99

FRUGAL FACT: *Find out what days your produce department marks down the different fruits and vegetables. Be sure to get mushrooms when you see them marked down and use them right away. If you want to make this hearty panini during the* *winter months, simply sauté the onions and mushrooms in a skillet, then use a waffle iron, quesadilla maker, electric griddle, or panini maker to make the sandwiches.*

Hawaiian Island Panini

1 loaf French bread ($.99)

1 tablespoon spicy mustard ($.05)

1 can (18 ounces) pineapple
    slices ($.99)

6 ounces sliced ham deli meat ($2)

4 slices Swiss cheese ($.75)

Slice the French bread loaf horizontally in half and then into 4 sections. Spread the spicy mustard onto one or both cut sides of the bread.

To each section, or sandwich, add 1 pineapple slice, 2 slices of ham, and 1 slice of Swiss cheese.

Preheat a skillet, electric griddle, panini press, or waffle iron. Place the sandwiches onto the hot appliance or skillet and press together. If using a skillet, flip the sandwich and press down with a potato masher or large spatula.

Serve Hawaiian Island Panini warm.

Makes 4 panini

Cost $4.78

FRUGAL FACT: *Make mini panini when you see a good sale price and/or a coupon matchup for the smaller sweet Hawaiian rolls.*

FIVE

Chicken and Turkey
One-Dish Dinners

BBQ Chicken and Cornbread Skillet Bake

2 boneless, skinless chicken breasts, about 1 pound, cut into bite-size pieces ($1.88)

1 small yellow onion, chopped ($.20)

6 carrot sticks, peeled and chopped ($.60)

1 bottle (6 ounces) BBQ sauce ($.49)

CORNBREAD TOPPING

1½ cups all-purpose flour ($.30)

1½ cups yellow cornmeal ($.52)

1 cup sugar ($.10)

1 tablespoon baking powder ($.10)

1 teaspoon salt

2 eggs ($.20)

1½ cups milk ($.15)

½ cup canola or vegetable oil ($.20)

2 tablespoons honey ($.05)

Preheat the oven to 350 degrees.

In a 12-inch cast-iron skillet, sauté the chicken pieces with the onion and carrots over medium-high heat. Once the chicken pieces have cooked through, reduce the heat to medium-low, stir in the BBQ sauce and let simmer for 5 to 7 minutes.

In a mixing bowl, whisk together the flour, cornmeal, sugar, baking powder, and salt. Add the egg, milk, oil, and honey and whisk until a smooth batter forms, about 2 minutes.

Pour the cornbread batter over the top of the chicken in the skillet and let cook for about 2 minutes, or until the cornbread batter begins to set along the edges of the skillet.

Transfer the skillet to the preheated oven and bake for 18 to 20 minutes until cornbread has baked through and begun to turn golden on top. Using heavy-duty oven mitts, carefully remove the skillet from the oven; the handle will be very hot. Let cool slightly before serving.

Serve BBQ Chicken and Cornbread Skillet Bake warm.

Makes 4 servings

Cost $4.79

FRUGAL FACT: *My "never-pay-more-than" price for a bottle of BBQ sauce is $.49.*

FREEZER FRIENDLY

Chicken Succotash

1 bag (10 ounces) frozen lima beans ($.80)

1 bag (10 ounces) frozen corn kernels ($.80)

2 garlic cloves, crushed ($.05)

1 tablespoon extra-virgin olive oil ($.05)

1 can (15 ounces) diced tomatoes, drained ($.20)

¼ cup sour cream ($.25)

Salt and pepper

2 cups cooked, shredded chicken ($1.50)

Bread and butter ($.50)

In a large 12-inch skillet or sauté pan, sauté the beans, corn, and garlic in the olive oil over medium-high heat. Once the beans and corn have cooked and the liquid has evaporated, add the diced tomatoes and the sour cream. Season the sauce with salt and pepper to taste.

Stir in the shredded chicken and let simmer for 5 to 7 minutes.

Serve Chicken Succotash with bread and butter.

Makes 4 servings

Cost $4.15

FRUGAL FACT: *You can substitute one 15-ounce can canned corn kernels for the frozen corn kernels or use the kernels from 2 ears of fresh corn.*

Skillet Jambalaya

....

½ pound boneless, skinless chicken
  breast, cut into 1-inch pieces ($1)
½ pound Italian sausage links, sliced
  into ½-inch rounds ($1.49)
1 tablespoon extra-virgin olive
  oil ($.05)
2 cups frozen chopped onion ($.80)
1 cup frozen chopped green bell
  pepper ($.40)

2 celery stalks, chopped ($.20)
1 can (15 ounces) diced tomatoes,
  with their juices ($.20)
1 tablespoon Creole seasoning
  ($.12)
1½ cups white rice ($.30)
2 to 2¼ cups hot water

In a large 12-inch skillet or sauté pan, brown the chicken pieces and the sausage in the olive oil over medium-high heat. Add the onion, bell pepper, and celery and cook with the chicken and sausage for 5 to 7 minutes.

Stir in the diced tomatoes and Creole seasoning and bring to a boil. Stir in the rice and enough of the water to cover the rice. Stir and press the rice down into the liquid. Cover the skillet, reduce the heat to low, and cook the rice for 18 to 20 minutes until tender. Stir once while the rice is cooking, quickly replacing the lid to keep the steam from escaping.

When the rice is tender, remove the skillet from the heat and let cool slightly before serving.

Serve Skillet Jambalaya warm.

Makes 4 servings

Cost $4.56

FRUGAL FACT: *For the perfect make-ahead meal: Place the chicken pieces, sausage slices, onions, celery, diced tomatoes, and seasoning into a gallon-size plastic freezer* *bag and freeze raw. To defrost, place in the refrigerator overnight. To cook, place the contents of the freezer bag into a large 12-inch skillet or sauté pan and sauté until the chicken and sausage are cooked through, then add the rice and liquid and follow the directions above from there.*

FREEZER FRIENDLY

Thai Chicken with Noodles

1 tablespoon extra-virgin olive
  oil ($.05)
2 boneless, skinless chicken breasts,
  about 1 pound, cut into bite-size
  pieces ($1.88)
1 bag (12 ounces) frozen stir-fry
  vegetables ($.80)

2 garlic cloves, crushed ($.05)
2 teaspoons lime juice ($.02)
2 teaspoons curry powder ($.10)
8 ounces cooked thin spaghetti
  ($.25)

In a large 12-inch skillet or wok, heat the olive oil, add the chicken pieces and sauté for 7 to 9 minutes until they are cooked through. Add the stir-fry vegetables, garlic, lime juice, and curry powder and sauté until the vegetables have defrosted and cooked through.

Toss in the cooked thin spaghetti and let cook with the sauce and the veggies for 2 to 3 minutes. Remove from the heat and serve warm from the skillet.

Serve Thai Chicken with Noodles.

Makes 4 servings

Cost $3.15

FRUGAL FACT: *Repurpose leftover thin spaghetti into a completely different kind of pasta dinner the next night, or two nights later, if you prefer not to enjoy the same pasta dish two nights in a row.*

Mango Chicken with Roasted Zucchini

....

2 boneless, skinless, chicken breasts, about 1 pound ($1.88)

1 small red onion, diced ($.40)

2 small zucchini, about 1 pound, cut into ½-inch rounds ($.79)

1 mango, peeled, seeded, and diced ($.99)

1 can (15 ounces) diced tomatoes, with their juices ($.20)

1 teaspoon extra-virgin olive oil ($.02)

Bread and butter ($.50)

Preheat the oven to 400 degrees.

Place the chicken breasts in the bottom of a roasting pan and season with salt and pepper. Scatter the onion, zucchini, and mango around the chicken. Then pour the diced tomatoes over the top. Gently toss the vegetables and fruit all together in the roasting pan.

Drizzle the olive oil over the top. Roast in the preheated oven for 45 to 50 minutes until the chicken is cooked through and the vegetables are tender. Slice the chicken before serving.

Serve Mango Chicken with Roasted Zucchini with bread and butter.

Makes 4 servings

Cost $4.78

FRUGAL FACT: *Add this recipe to your next batch-cooking day as a "make-ahead meal." Place all the ingredients in a plastic freezer bag and stash it in the freezer. Let defrost in the refrigerator overnight before roasting as directed above.*

MAKE-AHEAD MEAL

Smothered Chicken and Okra Bake

....

2 boneless, skinless chicken breasts, about 1 pound, cut into bite-size pieces ($1.88)

Salt and pepper

1½ cups brown rice ($.60)

1 bag (12 ounces) frozen cut okra ($.80)

1½ cups frozen mixed vegetables ($.60)

1 can (15 ounces) diced tomatoes, with their juices ($.20)

2 tablespoons Creole seasoning ($.25)

3 cups hot water

1 cup shredded cheddar cheese ($.67)

Preheat the oven to 350 degrees. Grease a 9 × 13-inch glass baking dish with nonstick cooking spray.

Place the chicken pieces in the prepared baking dish. Season with a few dashes of salt and pepper. Add the rice to the dish.

In a mixing bowl, combine the okra and mixed vegetables. Toss with the diced tomatoes and the Creole seasoning. Pour the vegetable mixture over the top of the rice and chicken in the baking dish. Add the hot water and cover the baking dish tightly with aluminum foil.

Bake in the preheated oven for 1 hour to 1 hour and 15 minutes until the rice is tender. Remove the foil from the baking dish and sprinkle the cheese over the chicken, rice, and vegetables. Return to the oven and bake, uncovered, for 10 to 15 minutes until the cheese has melted.

Serve Smothered Chicken and Okra Bake.

Makes 4 servings

Cost $5.00

FRUGAL FACT: *This "dump-and-bake" meal is perfect for a busy afternoon around the house. Just get it into the oven an hour before you want to eat and let the oven take care of the rest.*

FREEZER FRIENDLY

Baked Honey-Mustard Chicken

4 boneless, skinless chicken thighs, about 1¼ pounds, cut into 1-inch pieces ($2.49)

1 red bell pepper, seeded and diced ($1)

1 green bell pepper, seeded and diced ($.59)

Salt and pepper

¼ cup honey ($.10)

3 tablespoons prepared spicy brown mustard ($.15)

1 tablespoon vinegar ($.05)

1½ cups white rice ($.30)

2½ cups hot water

Preheat the oven to 350 degrees. Grease a 9 × 13-inch glass baking dish with nonstick cooking spray.

Place the cut chicken thigh pieces into the prepared baking dish. Add the red and green bell peppers and sprinkle the top with salt and pepper.

In a small mixing bowl, whisk together the honey, prepared mustard, and vinegar. Pour over the chicken and peppers and toss lightly.

Sprinkle the rice over the top of the chicken and pepper mixture and pour over the hot water. Cover the baking dish tightly with aluminum foil.

Bake in the preheated oven for 45 to 50 minutes until the chicken and rice have cooked through. Fluff the rice lightly with a fork before serving.

Serve Baked Honey-Mustard Chicken.

Makes 4 servings

Cost $4.68

FRUGAL FACT: *My "never-pay-more-than" price for boneless, skinless chicken thighs is $1.99 per pound or less.*

FREEZER FRIENDLY

Caribbean Chicken and Rice Bake

2 boneless, skinless chicken breasts, about 1 pound, cut into bite-size pieces ($1.88)

1 green bell pepper, seeded and cut into bite-size pieces ($.59)

1 mango, seeded, peeled, and cut into bite-size pieces ($.99)

1½ cups brown rice ($.60)

½ teaspoon ground cumin ($.03)

½ teaspoon chili powder ($.03)

4 cups hot water

½ teaspoon garlic salt ($.03)

Pepper

Preheat the oven to 350 degrees. Grease a 9 × 13-inch glass baking dish with nonstick cooking spray.

Toss together the chicken pieces, bell pepper, and mango in the prepared dish. Sprinkle the rice, cumin, and chili powder over the mixture and toss again. Pour the hot water over the mixture. Sprinkle with garlic salt and pepper over the bake. Cover the baking dish tightly with aluminum foil.

Bake in the preheated oven for 1 hour to 1 hour and 10 minutes. Fluff the rice lightly with a fork before serving.

Serve Caribbean Chicken and Rice Bake.

Makes 4 servings

Cost $4.15

FRUGAL FACT: *If you find a great deal on mangoes, then cut them up and freeze the flesh. The frozen mango could be used for this recipe, or in smoothies.*

FREEZER FRIENDLY

Swiss Chicken and Rice Casserole

....

2 boneless, skinless chicken breasts, about 1 pound, cut into bite-size pieces ($1.88)

1 teaspoon paprika ($.10)

Garlic salt and pepper

1 red bell pepper, seeded and diced ($1)

1 can (15 ounces) petite diced tomatoes, drained ($.20)

1½ cups brown rice ($.60)

3 cups hot water

1½ cups shredded Swiss cheese ($1)

Preheat the oven to 350 degrees. Grease a 9 × 13-inch glass baking dish with non-stick cooking spray.

Add the chicken pieces to the bottom of the prepared baking dish. Sprinkle the paprika, garlic salt, and pepper over the chicken pieces. Add the bell pepper and diced tomatoes to the chicken and toss gently.

Sprinkle the rice over the top of the chicken mixture. Pour the hot water over the mixture and gently press all the rice under the water. Cover the baking dish tightly with aluminum foil.

Bake in the preheated oven for 55 to 60 minutes. Remove the foil and sprinkle the shredded cheese over the baked chicken and rice. Return the dish to the oven and bake, uncovered, for 10 to 15 minutes more until the cheese has melted.

Serve Swiss Chicken and Rice Casserole.

Makes 4 servings

Cost $4.78

FRUGAL FACT: *Spend less on the cheese by purchasing a block of Swiss cheese. Because Swiss cheese is a softer cheese, it's best to put it in the freezer for 30 minutes before shredding or grating it.*

FREEZER FRIENDLY

Spicy Orange Chicken Bake

....

2 boneless skinless chicken breasts, about 1 pound, cut into bite-size pieces ($1.88)

6 carrots, peeled and chopped ($.60)

1 teaspoon finely grated orange zest

¼ cup freshly squeezed orange juice (about 1 navel orange) ($.50)

1 can (15 ounces) tomato sauce ($.20)

3 tablespoons brown sugar ($.04)

½ teaspoon garlic powder ($.03)

½ teaspoon ground cinnamon ($.03)

½ teaspoon ground ginger ($.03)

½ teaspoon crushed red pepper flakes ($.03)

1 cup brown rice ($.40)

1¼ cups hot water

Preheat the oven to 350 degrees. Grease a 9 × 13-inch glass baking dish with non-stick cooking spray.

In the prepared baking dish, gently toss together the chicken pieces, carrots, orange zest, orange juice, tomato sauce, brown sugar, garlic powder, cinnamon, ginger, and red pepper flakes until well combined.

Stir in the rice and the hot water. Cover the baking dish tightly with aluminum foil.

Bake in the preheated oven for 1 hour and 15 minutes until the rice is tender. Fluff the rice with a fork and let cool slightly before serving.

Serve Spicy Orange Chicken Bake.

Makes 4 servings

Cost $3.74

FRUGAL FACT: *This is the perfect dish to add to the meal plan when you find that you have just 1 orange left in the fruit drawer in the fridge.*

FREEZER FRIENDLY

Chicken Fajita Casserole

....

1 pound chicken tenderloins, cut into
  1-inch pieces ($1.88)
1 can (15 ounces) crushed
  tomatoes ($.20)
2 tablespoons Homemade Taco
  Seasoning (page 266) ($.20)

1 bag (12 ounces) frozen pepper and
  onion blend ($.80)
10 corn tortillas ($.69)
1½ cups shredded pepper Jack cheese
  blend ($1)

Preheat the oven to 350 degrees. Grease an 8 × 8-inch glass baking dish with nonstick cooking spray.

In a mixing bowl, toss together the chicken pieces, crushed tomatoes, taco seasoning, and pepper and onion blend.

Cover the bottom of the prepared baking dish with 3 or 4 corn tortillas. Spoon half of the chicken mixture on top of the tortillas. Sprinkle ½ cup of the shredded cheese on top. Then repeat the layering with the tortillas, chicken mixture, and the remaining tortillas and top with the remaining cheese.

Bake in the preheated oven for 35 to 40 minutes until the chicken pieces have cooked through and the cheese is melted and golden. Let cool slightly before cutting and serving.

Serve Chicken Fajita Casserole.

Makes 4 servings

Cost $4.77

FRUGAL FACT: *My "never-pay-more-than" price for chicken tenderloins is $1.88 per pound.*

FREEZER FRIENDLY

Chicken Cashew Bake

6 bone-in, skin-on chicken thighs, about 2 pounds ($1.99)

1 teaspoon curry powder ($.05)

1 teaspoon ground cumin ($.05)

Salt and pepper

1 cup white rice ($.20)

1 can (15 ounces) diced tomatoes, with their juices ($.20)

4 carrots, peeled and chopped ($.40)

1¾ cups water

1 cup cashews, chopped ($1)

Preheat the oven to 350 degrees. Grease a 9 × 13-inch glass baking dish with nonstick cooking spray.

Place the chicken thighs in the prepared baking dish.

In a small mixing bowl, mix together the curry powder, cumin, and salt and pepper to taste. Pull the skin back on the chicken thighs, divide the spice mix evenly among all the chicken thighs and sprinkle under the skin, directly on the meat. Fold the skin back down and sprinkle each thigh on top with a little more salt and pepper.

Spread the rice, diced tomatoes, and carrots around the chicken in the baking dish. Pour in the hot water. Cover tightly with aluminum foil

Bake in the preheated oven for 55 to 60 minutes until the rice is tender. Fluff the rice with a fork and let cool slightly before serving.

Sprinkle the chopped cashews over the chicken and rice in each serving bowl.

Serve Chicken Cashew Bake.

Makes 4 servings

Cost $3.89

FRUGAL FACT: *My "never-pay-more-than price" for bone-in, skin-on chicken thighs is $.99 per pound.*

Santa Fe Chicken and Rice Casserole

1 pound chicken tenderloins, cut into
    1-inch pieces ($1.99)
1½ cups brown rice ($.60)
1 small yellow onion, chopped ($.20)
1 red bell pepper, seeded and
    diced ($1)
1 can (15 ounces) corn kernels,
    drained ($.50)

2 cups cooked black beans
    (page 16) ($.40)
1½ teaspoons ground cumin
    ($.08)
3 cups hot water
Salt and pepper
½ teaspoon crushed red pepper
    flakes ($.03)

Preheat the oven to 350 degrees. Grease a 9 × 13-inch glass baking dish with nonstick cooking spray.

In the prepared baking dish, gently toss together the chicken, rice, onion, bell pepper, corn, beans, and cumin until well combined. Carefully pour in the hot water. Season with salt, black pepper, and the red pepper flakes. Cover the baking dish tightly with aluminum foil.

Bake in the preheated oven for 1 hour and 15 minutes until the rice is tender. Fluff the rice with a fork and let cool slightly before serving.

Serve Santa Fe Chicken and Rice Casserole.

Makes 4 servings

Cost $4.80 (Note: The cost will change with the substitution of canned beans.)

FRUGAL FACT: *Not every casserole calls for cheese, and cheese isn't necessary to make a rice bake taste delicious! This Santa Fe Chicken and Rice casserole is loaded with flavor and the perfect casserole for those with dairy food allergies or lactose intolerance.*

Mango Chicken Curry Bake

....

2 boneless, skinless chicken breasts, about 1 pound total, cut into bite-size pieces ($1.88)

2 mangoes, seeded, peeled, and diced ($1.98)

1 tablespoon curry powder ($.15)

1 teaspoon ground ginger ($.05)

Salt and pepper

½ cup light coconut milk ($.50)

1 cup brown rice ($.40)

1½ cups hot water

Preheat the oven to 350 degrees. Grease a 9 × 13-inch glass baking dish with nonstick cooking spray.

Gently toss the chicken pieces, mango, curry powder, and ginger in the prepared baking dish. Season with a little salt and pepper.

Pour the coconut milk and rice evenly over the chicken and mango mixture. Then pour in the hot water. Stir the ingredients together gently and cover the dish tightly with aluminum foil.

Bake in the preheated oven for 1 hour and 15 minutes, until the chicken has cooked through and the rice is tender. Fluff the rice with a fork and let cool slightly before serving.

Serve Mango Chicken Curry Bake.

Makes 4 servings

Cost $4.96

FRUGAL FACT: *The extra coconut milk can be stored in a plastic storage container in the refrigerator for up to a week, or in the freezer for up to 3 months.*

FREEZER FRIENDLY

Turkey and Corn Enchilada Casserole

1 can (15 ounces) crushed
  tomatoes ($.20)

½ small yellow onion, finely
  chopped ($.15)

1 garlic clove, crushed ($.03)

1 tablespoon chili powder ($.15)

1 teaspoon ground cumin ($.05)

½ pound ground turkey,
  cooked ($1.40)

1 can (15 ounces) corn kernels ($.50)

2 cups cooked black beans ($.40)

10 corn tortillas ($.69)

2 cups shredded Mexican blend or
  Monterey Jack cheese ($1.25)

Preheat the oven to 350 degrees. Grease a 9 × 13-inch glass baking dish with non-stick cooking spray.

In a mixing bowl, combine the crushed tomatoes, onion, and garlic. Stir in the chili powder and the cumin.

Mix in the cooked ground turkey, corn, and beans. Place 5 of the corn tortillas in the bottom of the prepared baking dish. You may have to tear the fifth tortilla to cover the middle or edge. Spoon the turkey, corn, and bean mixture over the tortillas. Sprinkle half the shredded cheese over the mixture. Top with the remaining 5 corn tortillas, covering as much of the mixture as you can. Sprinkle with the remaining shredded cheese.

Bake in the preheated oven for 25 to 30 minutes until the cheese begins to turn golden.

Serve Turkey and Corn Enchilada Casserole.

Makes 4 servings

Cost $4.82 (Note: The cost will change with the substitution of canned beans.)

FRUGAL FACT: *If you purchased your turkey in a 1-pound package, use the remaining ½ pound of cooked ground turkey in place of ground beef in your favorite spaghetti sauce, meat loaf, or meatballs recipe.*

Stovetop Chicken, Broccoli, and Rice Casserole

6 tablespoons butter ($.60)

6 tablespoons all-purpose flour ($.07)

2 cups milk ($.20)

1 teaspoon garlic powder ($.05)

1 teaspoon salt

1 teaspoon pepper

1 bag (12 ounces) frozen broccoli florets ($.80)

2 boneless, skinless chicken breasts, about 1 pound, cut into bite-size pieces ($1.88)

1 cup white rice ($.20)

1 cup hot water

½ cup grated Parmesan cheese ($.50)

In a large pot or Dutch oven, melt the butter over medium heat. Whisk in the flour and then slowly pour in the milk, and cook, whisking constantly, for at least 1 minute. Reduce the heat to medium and cook, whisking often until the sauce begins to bubble and thicken. Add the garlic powder, salt, and pepper.

Once the sauce has thickened, add the broccoli florets, chicken pieces, rice, and hot water and stir to combine. Cover and simmer for 15 to 20 minutes until the broccoli florets are tender, the chicken has cooked through, and the rice is tender. Sprinkle the grated cheese over the cooked rice and remove the pot from the heat. Let cool slightly before serving.

Serve Stovetop Chicken, Broccoli, and Rice Casserole.

Makes 4 servings

Cost $4.30

FRUGAL FACT: *Making your own white sauce brings a much fuller and delicious flavor to your meal.*

Curried Chicken Quinoa with Peas

1 tablespoon extra-virgin olive
   oil ($.05)
1 pound boneless, skinless chicken
   thighs, cut into bite-size
   pieces ($1.99)
1 small red onion, chopped ($.40)
2 garlic cloves, crushed ($.05)
1 can (15 ounces) petite diced
   tomatoes, with their juices ($.20)

1 tablespoon curry powder ($.10)
1½ teaspoons chili powder ($.05)
1 teaspoon ground nutmeg ($.10)
2 cups hot water
1 cup white quinoa ($.80)
1 bag (12 ounces) frozen peas ($.80)
Salt and pepper

In a large pot or Dutch oven over medium-high heat, warm the olive oil. Add the chicken pieces, onion, and garlic and sauté for 10 minutes, or until the chicken pieces have cooked through.

Stir in the diced tomatoes, curry powder, chili powder, and nutmeg. Stir until combined and let cook for about 5 minutes.

Pour in the hot water and bring to a boil. Stir in the quinoa, return to a rolling boil. Reduce the heat to medium-low, cover, and cook for 20 minutes. Five minutes before the end of the cooking, stir in the frozen peas. Season to taste with salt and pepper. Reduce the heat to low and keep warm until ready to serve.

Serve Curried Chicken Quinoa with Peas.

Makes 4 servings

Cost $4.54

FRUGAL FACT: *Stock up on the flavorful boneless, skinless chicken thighs anytime you see their price dip below $2 per pound. Purchase enough to store in your freezer to last until the next sale cycle.*

Spicy Chicken Chofan

1 tablespoon extra-virgin olive oil ($.05)

2 boneless, skinless chicken breasts, about 1 pound, cut into bite-size pieces ($1.88)

1 tablespoon Homemade Taco Seasoning (page 266) ($.10)

1 cup brown rice ($.40)

2¾ cups hot water

1 can (10 ounces) diced tomatoes with green chilies, with their juices ($.50)

1 can (15 ounces) corn kernels, drained ($.50)

Salt and pepper

2 avocados, seeded and sliced ($1.50)

In a large pot or Dutch oven, heat the olive oil over medium-high heat. Add the chicken pieces and sauté along with the taco seasoning for 4 to 6 minutes until cooked through.

Add the rice and the hot water. Stir in the diced tomatoes with green chilies and the corn, season with salt and pepper to taste, and bring to a boil. Reduce the heat to medium, cover, and cook for 45 to 50 minutes until the rice is tender. Fluff the rice lightly with a fork before serving.

Serve Spicy Chicken Chofan topped with sliced avocados.

Makes 4 servings

Cost $4.93

FRUGAL FACT: *Chofan is the Dominican word for "pilaf," and this is a traditional Dominican chofan, using ingredients straight from the pantry.*

One-Dish Chicken Spaghetti

1 pound spaghetti ($.50)

2 boxes (10 ounces, each) frozen chopped spinach ($1)

1 can (15 ounces) diced tomatoes with roasted garlic, with their juices ($.20)

1 teaspoon dried Italian seasoning ($.05)

2 cups cooked, shredded chicken ($1.50)

¼ cup grated Parmesan cheese ($.25)

In a large pot or Dutch oven, boil the spaghetti according to the directions on the package. Drain and set aside in the colander while you prepare the sauce.

Meanwhile, cook the frozen spinach in the microwave, according to package directions. Drain off the liquid from the spinach, but don't squeeze it completely dry.

Return the pot or Dutch oven to the stovetop and add the diced tomatoes, Italian seasoning, drained, cooked spinach, and the chicken. Stir until well combined. Season the sauce with salt and pepper to taste.

Return the spaghetti to the pot and toss well to combine with the sauce. Sprinkle with grated cheese just before serving.

Serve One-Dish Chicken Spaghetti.

Makes 4 servings

Cost $3.50

FRUGAL FACT: *The best price for a 10-ounce box of frozen spinach is $1. Paired with a coupon, it can be purchased for as little as $.50 per box. Canned spinach can also be found for $.50 per can or less. If you have canned spinach on hand, you can use it for this recipe; drain it well before adding it to the sauce.*

Braised Chicken with Radishes, Carrots, and Red Potatoes

....

1 tablespoon extra-virgin olive
   oil ($.05)

2 split chicken breasts, about 1¾
   pounds ($1.75)

Salt and pepper

1 cup hot water

½ teaspoon lemon zest

Juice of 1 lemon ($.25)

4 carrots, peeled and cut into
   1-inch pieces ($.40)

2 celery stalks, cut into 1-inch
   pieces ($.20)

1 small red onion, diced ($.40)

½ pound radishes, stems removed,
   trimmed, and halved ($.50)

6 medium red potatoes,
   quartered ($.80)

In a large pot or Dutch oven over medium-high heat, warm the olive oil. Season the chicken breasts with a little salt and pepper and brown for 2 minutes on each side. Remove the chicken breasts from the pot and set them on a plate.

Over high heat, deglaze the pot with the hot water. Zest the lemon, then squeeze the lemon juice into the pot. Add the carrots, celery, onion, radishes, potatoes, and lemon zest and toss to combine. Reduce the heat to medium and let cook for 3 to 5 minutes. Return the chicken breasts to the pot, and nestle them into the vegetables. Cover the pot tightly and braise over medium heat for 45 to 50 minutes until the chicken has cooked through. The cooking time may vary depending on the thickness of the split chicken breast. Slice the chicken before serving.

Serve Braised Chicken with Radishes, Carrots, and Red Potatoes.

Makes 4 servings

Cost $4.35

FRUGAL FACT: *My "never-pay-more-than" price for split chicken breasts is $.99 per pound.*

Chicken and Vegetable Curry

1 tablespoon extra-virgin olive oil ($.05)

2 garlic cloves, crushed ($.05)

2 boneless, skinless chicken breasts, about 1 pound, cut into bite-size pieces ($1.88)

½ cup light coconut milk ($.50)

1 bag (12 ounces) frozen stir-fry vegetables ($.80)

4 medium Idaho potatoes, peeled and diced ($.60)

½ cup hot water

2 tablespoons curry powder ($.30)

1 teaspoon ground ginger ($.05)

Salt and pepper

In a large pot or Dutch oven over medium-high heat, warm the olive oil. Add the garlic and chicken pieces and sauté for 7 to 9 minutes until the chicken has cooked through.

Stir in the coconut milk, stir-fry vegetables, potatoes, and hot water. Stir in the curry powder, ginger, and salt and pepper to taste and bring to a boil. Reduce to a simmer, cover, and cook for 15 to 20 minutes until the potatoes are tender. Let cool slightly before serving.

Serve Chicken and Vegetable Curry.

Makes 4 servings

Cost $4.23

FRUGAL FACT: *Stock up on coconut milk when you see it on sale for less than $1.50 per can. And popular name brands release coupons several times each year, so be sure to take advantage of the coupon savings, too.*

MAKE-AHEAD MEAL

Pan-Roasted Chicken with Garden Vegetables

1 tablespoon extra-virgin olive
   oil ($.05)

1 teaspoon red wine vinegar ($.02)

2 split chicken breasts, about
   2¼ pounds ($2.22)

2 cups water

2 carrots, peeled and cut into 1-inch
   pieces ($.20)

4 small red potatoes, quartered ($.80)

2 small zucchini, about 1 pound,
   cut into 1-inch rounds ($.79)

1 small yellow squash, about
   ½ pound, cut into 1-inch
   rounds ($.39)

¼ cup lemon juice ($.20)

1 teaspoon dried dill ($.10)

Salt and pepper

In a large pot or Dutch oven over medium-high heat, warm the olive oil and vinegar. Add the chicken and sauté for 2 minutes on each side, then add the water. Add the carrots, potatoes, zucchini, and yellow squash. Sprinkle the lemon juice and dill over the top and season with salt and pepper.

Bring the liquid to a boil, then reduce the heat to medium, cover, and cook for 35 to 40 minutes until the chicken has cooked through. The cooking time may vary depending on the thickness of the chicken breast. Let cool slightly before serving.

Serve Pan-Roasted Chicken with Garden Vegetables.

Makes 4 servings

Cost $4.77

FRUGAL FACT: *To make the most of your time in the kitchen, prepare the vegetables while the chicken is browning.*

MAKE-AHEAD MEAL

Coconut Ginger Chicken

1 tablespoon extra-virgin olive oil ($.05)

4 bone-in chicken thighs, about 2 pounds, skin removed ($1.99)

1 teaspoon garlic powder ($.05)

Salt and pepper

1 cup light coconut milk ($1)

2 cups hot water

1 teaspoon ground ginger ($.05)

2 teaspoons curry powder ($.10)

¾ cup white rice ($.15)

4 Granny Smith apples, peeled, cored, and diced ($1)

½ cup raisins, for garnish ($.37)

In a large pot or Dutch oven over medium-high heat, warm the olive oil, then add the chicken thighs and brown. While browning, season both sides of the chicken with garlic powder, salt, and pepper to taste.

When the chicken has browned, add the coconut milk and hot water, stir in the ginger and curry powder, and bring to a boil.

Add the rice, and return to a boil. Reduce the heat to low, cover, and simmer for 20 minutes, or until the rice is tender. After the rice has been cooking for 10 minutes, add the apples, cover, and finish cooking the rice for the remaining 10 minutes. Fluff the rice with a fork and let cook slightly before serving.

Serve Coconut Ginger Chicken garnished with raisins.

Makes 4 servings

Cost $4.77

FRUGAL FACT: *The best per-ounce price option for raisins will always be the larger bulk bags of raisins.*

MAKE-AHEAD MEAL

Slow Cooker Curried Coconut Chicken

1 can (15 ounces) light coconut milk ($1.50)

1 tablespoon curry powder ($.15)

½ teaspoon ground ginger ($.05)

Salt and pepper

½ teaspoon crushed red pepper flakes (optional) ($.03)

2 boneless, skinless chicken breasts, about 1 pound, cut into bite-size pieces ($1.88)

1 bag (12 ounces) frozen stir-fry vegetables ($.80)

1 cup white rice ($.20)

1 cup hot water

Shake the can of coconut milk vigorously before opening. Pour the coconut milk into the insert of a lightly greased 5-quart or larger slow cooker. Whisk to smooth out the coconut milk, if necessary. Whisk in the curry powder, ginger, and salt and black pepper to taste, and the red pepper flakes, if you wish it to be spicy.

Place the cut chicken pieces into the coconut milk and spoon some of the milk over the top of the chicken. Then add the stir-fry vegetables on top.

Set the slow cooker on high and cook for 6 hours, or on low and cook for 10 hours.

When there is about 1 hour remaining in the cooking cycle, add the rice to the slow cooker with the hot water and complete the cooking cycle.

Serve the Slow Cooker Curried Coconut Chicken.

Makes 4 servings

Cost $4.61

FRUGAL FACT: *You can substitute brown rice for the white rice, but add it to the slow cooker 2 hours before the cooking cycle is complete, and increase the hot water to 1½ cups.*

Slow Cooker Rosemary Chicken with Red Potatoes and Green Beans

3 rosemary sprigs ($.25)

2 pounds bone-in chicken thighs ($1.99)

6 small red potatoes, quartered ($1.20)

1 small yellow onion, diced ($.20)

1 tablespoon extra-virgin olive oil ($.05)

1 teaspoon garlic powder ($.05)

Salt and pepper

1 pound green beans, stems removed ($.99)

Using a sharp knife, crush the leaves of the rosemary sprig. This allows the aromatic oils to release as it cooks. Place the rosemary sprigs around the edges of the bottom of a 5-quart or larger slow cooker.

Arrange the chicken thighs in the bottom of the slow cooker. Spread the potatoes over the top of the chicken. Drizzle the olive oil over the top of the chicken and potatoes, and then season with the garlic powder and salt and pepper.

Set the slow cooker on low and cook for 8 hours. When there is 1 hour remaining in the cooking cycle, place the green beans on top of the chicken and potatoes to steam them. Complete the cooking cycle.

Serve Slow Cooker Rosemary Chicken with Red Potatoes and Green Beans.

Makes 4 servings

Cost $4.73

FRUGAL FACT: *This is the perfect meal to use up the rosemary from your garden or patio planter.*

MAKE-AHEAD MEAL

Chipotle Chicken Tacos

1¼ pounds boneless, skinless chicken thighs ($2.48)

1 small yellow onion, finely chopped ($.20)

10 corn taco shells ($.99)

1 can (15 ounces) corn kernels, warmed ($.50)

1 can (10 ounces) diced tomatoes with green chilies, with their juices ($.50)

1 tablespoon chipotle chili powder ($.10)

Sour cream for serving ($.10)

To a 5-quart or larger slow cooker, add the boneless, skinless chicken thighs. Spread the onion and diced tomatoes with green chilies around the chicken thighs. Sprinkle the chipotle chili powder over the chicken and tomatoes. Set the slow cooker on high and cook for 4 hours, or on low and cook for 8 hours.

Once the cooking cycle is complete, use two forks to pull apart the chicken meat and toss it together with the tomatoes. Strain any extra liquid from the chicken before adding it to the tacos.

Stuff each taco with the chipotle chicken, warmed corn, and add a dollop of sour cream.

Serve Chipotle Chicken Tacos.

Makes 10 tacos

Cost $4.87

FRUGAL FACT: *My never-pay-more-than price for corn taco shells is $.99 for a box of 10. They can sometimes be purchased for as little as $.50 with the right sale price and coupon matchup.*

Slow Cooker Chicken Soft Tacos

2 boneless, skinless chicken breasts,
    about 1 pound ($1.88)

1 can (10 ounces) diced tomatoes with
    green chilies, with their juices ($.50)

1 bag (12 ounces) frozen pepper and
    onion blend ($.80)

1 teaspoon ground cumin ($.05)

Salt and pepper

8 soft taco-size tortillas ($1)

1 cup shredded iceberg lettuce ($.25)

½ cup shredded cheddar cheese ($.32)

Sour cream for serving ($.10)

Add the chicken breasts, diced tomatoes with green chilies, pepper and onion blend, cumin, and salt and pepper to the insert of a slow cooker. Set the slow cooker on high and cook for 4 hours, or on low and cook for 8 hours.

Once the chicken has cooked, drain the liquid from the chicken, peppers, and tomatoes and shred the chicken meat with a fork.

Place the shredded chicken into each of the tortillas and add shredded lettuce, a pinch of shredded cheese, and a dollop of sour cream. Roll up the tortillas before serving.

Serve Slow Cooker Chicken Soft Tacos.

Makes 4 servings

Cost $4.90

FRUGAL FACT: *My never-pay-more-than price for tortillas is $1.29 for a package of 10. When on sale, or below this price, stock up and freeze a few extra packages.*

Chicken, Zucchini, and Feta Grill Packets

2 large boneless, skinless chicken
    breasts, about 1¼ pounds, halved
    ($2.08)
1 tablespoon extra-virgin olive
    oil ($.05)
1 tablespoon red wine vinegar ($.05)
2 medium zucchini, about 1¼
    pounds, sliced ($.98)

1 can (15 ounces) diced tomatoes,
    drained ($.20)
1 teaspoon dried Italian
    seasoning ($.05)
Salt and pepper
2 ounces feta cheese ($.75)

4 slices Grilled Garlic Bread (page 268) ($.75)

Preheat the grill for indirect cooking over medium heat.

Place each of the chicken breast halves onto a piece of aluminum foil that is large enough to completely enclose the chicken and vegetables in a packet.

Drizzle a little olive oil and vinegar over the chicken. Add 8 to 10 slices of zucchini to each foil packet, and divide the tomatoes evenly among the grill packets. Sprinkle the contents of each grill packet with a little Italian seasoning and salt and pepper to taste.

Place the grill packets over indirect heat on the preheated grill and close the grill. Cook for 20 to 25 minutes until the chicken has cooked through. The cooking time may vary depending on the thickness of the chicken breasts.

Grill the garlic bread alongside the grill packets.

When cooked through, remove the grill packets and garlic bread from the grill. Open up each packet and sprinkle the feta cheese evenly over the chicken and vegetables.

Serve Chicken, Zucchini, and Feta Grill Packets with Grilled Garlic Bread.

Makes 4 servings

Cost $4.91

FRUGAL FACT: *A simple, no-mess, no-fuss dinner on the grill.*

MAKE-AHEAD MEAL

Pesto Chicken Grill Packets

2 large boneless, skinless chicken breasts, about 1¼ pounds, halved ($2.08)

1 tablespoon extra-virgin olive oil, divided ($.05)

1 tablespoon red wine vinegar, divided ($.05)

2 medium zucchini, about 1¼ pounds, sliced ($.98)

4 tablespoons pesto sauce ($.75)

¼ cup grated Parmesan cheese ($.25)

Salt and pepper

4 slices Grilled Garlic Bread (page 268) ($.75)

Preheat the grill for indirect cooking over medium heat.

Place each of the chicken breast halves onto a piece of aluminum foil that is large enough to completely enclose the chicken and vegetables in a packet.

Drizzle a little olive oil and vinegar over the chicken. Add 8 to 10 slices of zucchini to each foil packet, and then add 1 tablespoon of pesto sauce to each grill packet. Sprinkle a few teaspoons of the grated cheese and some salt and pepper over the contents of each grill packet.

Place the grill packets over indirect heat on the preheated grill and close the grill. Cook for 15 to 20 minutes until the chicken has cooked through. The cooking time may vary depending on the thickness of the chicken breasts.

Grill the garlic bread alongside the grill packets.

When the chicken has cooked through, remove the grill packets and garlic bread from the grill.

Serve Pesto Chicken Grill Packets with Grilled Garlic Bread.

Makes 4 servings

Cost $4.91

FRUGAL FACT: *You can dramatically reduce the overall cost of this meal by making your own pesto sauce using herbs from the garden or patio planter.*

MAKE-AHEAD MEAL

Chicken and Potatoes Grill-Fry

2 boneless, skinless chicken breasts, about 1 pound, cut into bite-size pieces ($1.88)

1 tablespoon extra-virgin olive oil ($.05)

2 teaspoons red wine vinegar ($.04)

2 tablespoons garlic and onion grill seasoning ($.10)

4 medium Idaho potatoes ($.60)

1 green bell pepper, seeded and diced ($.59)

1 white onion, diced ($.20)

Ketchup for serving ($.10)

Fresh fruit, such as watermelon slices or cantaloupe wedges ($.50)

Put the chicken pieces in a glass mixing bowl along with the olive oil, vinegar, and grill seasoning. Let marinate in the refrigerator for at least 30 minutes.

Microwave the potatoes for a few minutes before slicing to help them cook faster on the grill, and then cut them into bite-size pieces.

Toss the potatoes, bell pepper, and onion with the chicken pieces.

Place the mixture into a mesh or metal grill basket and cook for about 20 minutes, tossing and turning the chicken and vegetables occasionally until the chicken pieces have cooked through. Use caution and a heavy-duty oven mitt or glove as the grill basket handle will be very hot.

Serve Chicken and Potatoes Grill-Fry with ketchup and a side of fresh fruit.

Makes 4 servings

Cost $4.06

FRUGAL FACT: *A grill basket is like a skillet for the grill. They can be purchased for anywhere between $5 and $20 (page 50).*

MAKE-AHEAD MEAL

SIX

Beef One-Dish Dinners

Skillet Lasagna Florentine

1 pound ground beef ($1.49)

1 small yellow onion, chopped ($.20)

3 garlic cloves, crushed ($.08)

1 box (10 ounces) frozen chopped spinach, cooked and drained ($.50)

1 can (15 ounces) diced tomatoes, with their juices ($.20)

1 can (8 ounces) tomato sauce ($.33)

1 teaspoon dried Italian seasoning ($.05)

1½ cups hot water

4 lasagna noodles, cut into 1-inch pieces ($.30)

Salt and pepper

1 cup shredded mozzarella cheese ($.67)

In a large 12-inch skillet or sauté pan over medium-high heat, brown the ground beef with the onion and garlic. Drain off any excess fat and return the browned meat to the skillet.

Cook the spinach according to package directions and drain well.

Add the diced tomatoes, tomato sauce, and cooked, drained spinach to the ground beef. Stir in the Italian seasoning and bring to a simmer. Season with salt and pepper to taste.

To the meat-tomato mixture in the skillet, add the hot water and mix in the cut lasagna noodles. Cover the skillet with a tight-fitting lid and cook over medium heat for about 10 minutes, or until the lasagna noodles are al dente.

Sprinkle the shredded cheese over the top of the skillet lasagna and cook, uncovered, for about 5 minutes more, or until the cheese has melted.

Serve Skillet Lasagna Florentine warm from the stovetop.

Makes 4 servings

Cost $3.82

FRUGAL FACT: *Don't pay more than $.33 for an 8-ounce can of tomato sauce, which are on sale regularly at the national drugstore chains.*

FREEZER FRIENDLY

Sloppy Joe Skillet-Bake

1 pound ground beef ($1.49)

2 cans (15 ounces) tomato sauce ($.40)

¼ cup water

1 small zucchini, about ⅔ pound, chopped ($.50)

4 carrots, peeled and chopped ($.40)

4 teaspoons apple cider vinegar ($.10)

3 tablespoons prepared yellow mustard ($.15)

¼ cup brown sugar ($.06)

Salt and pepper

4 store-bought hamburger buns ($.50)

1 cup shredded cheddar cheese ($.67)

In a large ovenproof 12-inch skillet or sauté pan over medium high heat, brown the ground beef. Drain and return it to the skillet.

Stir in the tomato sauce and water, the zucchini, carrots, vinegar, mustard, brown sugar, and salt and pepper to taste. Let simmer over low heat for about 10 minutes.

Preheat the oven to 350 degrees.

Open up the hamburger buns and place them face down, covering the sloppy Joe mixture. Sprinkle with the shredded cheese and transfer the skillet into the preheated oven. Bake for 10 to 12 minutes until the cheese has melted.

Using heavy-duty oven mitts, carefully remove the skillet from the oven. Let cool slightly before serving. To serve, dish out the meat sauce with one or two of the buns over the top of the meat.

Serve Sloppy Joe Skillet-Bake.

Makes 4 servings

Cost $4.27

FRUGAL FACT: *Freeze the other 4 hamburger buns in the bag for another use. Use for bread pudding, a breakfast bake, or for mini pizzas or burgers later in the month.*

FREEZER FRIENDLY

Skillet Beef Stroganoff

1 tablespoon extra-virgin olive oil ($.05)

¾ pound beef stew meat ($1.49)

2 cups store-bought or Homemade Beef Broth (page 257) (free, if homemade)

1 can (4 ounces) sliced mushrooms ($.49)

1 cup sour cream ($1)

3 cups egg noodles, about 8 ounces ($.25)

1 cup hot water

Fresh fruit, such as cantaloupe wedges or orange slices ($.50)

In a large 12-inch skillet or sauté pan over medium-high heat, warm the olive oil. Add the beef stew meat and brown. Reduce the heat to medium-low, add the beef broth, mushrooms, and sour cream, and stir to combine. Simmer for 5 to 7 minutes.

Stir in the egg noodles and the hot water. Cover and simmer for 7 to 9 minutes more until the egg noodles are just cooked. Remove the skillet from the heat and serve immediately so that the noodles don't overcook.

Serve Skillet Beef Stroganoff with fresh fruit.

Makes 4 servings

Cost $3.78 (Note: The cost will change with the substitution of store-bought beef broth.)

FRUGAL FACT: *You can sign up to receive a weekly e-mail at 5dollardinners.com with the best food deals at the national drugstores, like the $.49 cans of mushrooms.*

Skillet Goulash with Spinach

1 pound ground beef ($1.49)

2 garlic cloves, crushed ($.05)

1 can (15 ounces) diced tomatoes, with their juices ($.20)

1 can (15 ounces) spinach, drained ($.50)

1 cup milk ($.10)

2 cups hot water

2 cups small shell pasta ($.25)

1 teaspoon all-purpose flour ($.01)

1 teaspoon dried Italian seasoning ($.05)

1 teaspoon paprika ($.10)

1 teaspoon onion powder ($.05)

Salt and pepper

½ cup sour cream ($.50)

¼ cup grated Parmesan cheese ($.25)

In a large 12-inch skillet or sauté pan over medium-high heat, brown the ground beef with the garlic. Drain and return it to the skillet.

Add the diced tomatoes, spinach, milk, water, and the pasta. Bring to a boil, reduce heat to medium-low, then stir in the flour, Italian seasoning, paprika, onion powder, and salt and pepper to taste. Cover and cook for 7 to 9 minutes until the pasta is al dente.

Remove the skillet from the heat and stir in the sour cream.

Serve Skillet Goulash with Spinach with a sprinkle of cheese for each serving bowl.

Makes 4 servings

Cost $3.55

FRUGAL FACT: *A kid favorite at our house, and a mom favorite as well because I can have this dinner on the table in 20 minutes.*

FREEZER FRIENDLY

Beef Fajita Skillet

1 tablespoon extra-virgin olive oil ($.05)

¾ pound beef for stir-fry or thinly sliced flank steak ($2.24)

1 tablespoon Homemade Taco Seasoning (page 266) ($.10)

1 bag (12 ounces) frozen pepper and onion blend ($.80)

1 can (15 ounces) diced tomatoes with garlic, with their juices ($.20)

6 corn tortillas, cut into 1-inch strips ($.65)

Salt and pepper

Fresh fruit, such as cantaloupe wedges or watermelon slices ($.50)

In a large 12-inch skillet or sauté pan over medium-high heat, warm the olive oil. Add the beef and sauté along with the taco seasoning for 5 to 8 minutes until the beef has cooked through.

Add the pepper and onion blend and diced tomatoes and cook for 3 to 4 minutes. Add the corn tortilla strips and stir into the sauce.

Reduce the heat to low, cover, and simmer for 1 to 2 minutes. Season with salt and pepper to taste. Remove from the heat and serve immediately.

Serve Beef Fajita Skillet with fresh fruit as a side dish.

Makes 4 servings

Cost $4.54

FRUGAL FACT: *My "never-pay-more-than" price for stir-fry beef is $2.99 per pound.*

Skillet Shells and Beef with Peppers

¾ pound ground beef ($1.12)

1 bag (12 ounces) frozen pepper and onion blend ($.80)

1 can (15 ounces) tomato sauce ($.20)

1 teaspoon dried Italian seasoning ($.05)

½ teaspoon garlic salt ($.01)

Black pepper

3 cups hot water

2 cups small shell pasta ($.25)

Fresh fruit, such as apple slices or orange wedges ($.50)

In a 12-inch skillet over medium-high heat, brown the ground beef. Drain and return it to the skillet.

Add the pepper and onion blend and the tomato sauce to the browned ground beef. Stir to combine and add the Italian seasoning, garlic salt, and a couple dashes of pepper. Bring the sauce to bubbling, then add 3 cups of hot water. Once the water is bubbling, stir in the pasta shells. Cover with a tight-fitting lid, reduce the heat to medium-high, and cook for 12 to 15 minutes until the pasta is al dente.

Uncover and let the sauce simmer until it reaches the desired consistency. The sauce will thicken slightly as it cools.

Serve Skillet Shells and Beef with Peppers with fresh fruit as a side dish.

Makes 4 servings

Cost $2.93

FRUGAL FACT: *If you'd like to add more pasta, simply add to the ground beef and tomato sauce mixture with a 3:2 water to pasta ratio.*

Savory Mac and Beef

1 pound ground beef ($1.49)

1 small red onion, chopped ($.40)

1 green bell pepper, seeded and
diced ($.59)

3 carrots, peeled and chopped ($.30)

2 celery stalks, chopped ($.20)

1 can (15 ounces) tomato sauce ($.20)

¼ cup Worcestershire sauce ($.10)

1½ cups elbow macaroni ($.20)

½ teaspoon dried Italian
seasoning ($.02)

Salt and pepper

Small side salad with store-bought or Homemade Basic Vinaigrette
(page 261) ($1.50)

In a large 12-inch skillet or sauté pan over medium-high heat, brown the ground beef with the onion. Drain and return the mixture to the skillet.

Add the bell pepper, carrots, and celery, and sauté over medium-high heat for 2 to 3 minutes.

Add the tomato sauce plus two 15-ounce cans' worth of water and the Worcestershire sauce. Stir in the elbow macaroni.

Season with the Italian seasoning and salt and pepper to taste and bring to a boil.

Reduce the heat to medium, cover, and let simmer for 12 to 15 minutes, or until the macaroni is al dente, stirring once. Let cool slightly before serving. The sauce will thicken as it cools.

Serve Savory Mac and Beef with a side salad.

Makes 4 servings

Cost $5.00

FRUGAL FACT: *Don't let those extra carrots go to waste. Peel and chop them and stash them in 1- or 2-cup portions in the freezer. Use them in recipes that call for chopped carrots that are cooked, as they will lose their crispness after being frozen. Simply toss in 1 cup frozen carrots to this recipe, and they will cook right in.*

Skillet Taco Pie

1 pound ground beef ($1.49)

1 can (15 ounces) corn kernels, drained ($.50)

1 can (10 ounces) diced tomatoes with green chilies, drained ($.50)

2 tablespoons Homemade Taco Seasoning (page 266) ($.20)

About 5 ounces tortilla chips, crushed ($.75)

1 cup shredded Mexican blend cheese ($.67)

1 avocado, sliced ($.75)

In a 12-inch cast-iron skillet over medium-high heat, brown the ground beef. Drain and return it to the skillet.

Reduce the heat to medium and add the corn and diced tomatoes with green chilies. Mix in the taco seasoning and let simmer for 3 to 4 minutes.

Take several handfuls of corn tortilla chips and crush them over the top of the beef mixture in the skillet; crush enough to cover the beef mixture with a thin layer. Then sprinkle the shredded cheese over the top of the crushed tortilla chips.

Reduce the heat to low, cover, and allow the cheese to melt. If necessary, cover with a lid, or a baking sheet if you don't have a tight-fitting lid, until the cheese has melted evenly.

Serve Skillet Taco Pie with avocado slices on top.

Makes 4 servings

Cost $4.86

FRUGAL FACT: *Because there are rarely good coupons for tortilla chips, expect the generic brand to have the better price.*

Beef and Zucchini Quesadilla Bake

1 pound ground beef, browned
($1.49)

1 small yellow onion, chopped
($.20)

2 medium zucchini, about 1¼
pounds, chopped ($.98)

2 tablespoons Homemade Taco
Seasoning (page 266) ($.20)

6 burrito-size flour tortillas ($.75)

2 cups shredded Mexican blend
cheese ($1.25)

Preheat the oven to 350 degrees. Grease a 9×9-inch glass baking dish with nonstick cooking spray.

In a mixing bowl, combine the browned ground beef, onion, zucchini, and taco seasoning.

Place 2 of the tortillas on the bottom of the prepared baking dish. Add about half of the meat and zucchini mixture on top of the tortillas. Sprinkle with half of the shredded cheese. Then repeat the layering with 2 more tortillas, the remaining beef mixture, and the remaining cheese. Top with the remaining 2 tortillas.

Bake in the preheated oven for 10 minutes. Then cover the baking dish with a piece of aluminum foil to prevent the top layer of tortillas from burning. Bake for 10 to 15 minutes more until the cheese has melted. Let cool slightly before cutting and serving.

Serve Beef and Zucchini Quesadilla Bake.

Makes 4 servings

Cost $4.87

FRUGAL FACT: *When you purchase a large number of packages of ground beef when on sale for $1.49 per pound or less, brown several pounds at once and then divide into 1-pound portions and freeze to use in future meals, such as this one.*

FREEZER FRIENDLY

Italian Shepherd's Pie

1 pound ground beef, browned
  ($1.49)
1 tablespoon dried Italian
  seasoning ($.15)
1 can (15 ounces) diced tomatoes,
  drained ($.20)

Salt and pepper
1 bag (12 ounces) frozen peppers
  and onion blend ($.80)
4 cups leftover mashed potatoes ($1)
2 cups shredded mozzarella
  cheese ($1.25)

Preheat the oven to 350 degrees. Grease a 9×13-inch glass baking dish with nonstick cooking spray.

Add the browned ground beef diced tomatoes, Italian seasonings, and salt and pepper to taste to the bottom of the prepared baking dish.

Spread the pepper and onion blend over the meat. Top with the leftover mashed potatoes and sprinkle the cheese over the top.

Bake in the preheated oven for 25 to 30 minutes until bubbly and the cheese has melted and begun to turn golden. Let cool slightly before cutting and serving.

Serve Italian Shepherd's Pie.

Makes 4 servings

Cost $4.89

FRUGAL FACT: *Not sure how much butter or milk you need for making mashed potatoes?! Use the Homemade Mashed Potatoes "Ratio" recipe on page 265.*

FREEZER FRIENDLY

Ten-Minute Shepherd's Pie

....

3 cups leftover spaghetti sauce ($1.50)

1 bag (12 ounces) frozen mixed
  vegetables ($.80)

4 cups leftover mashed potatoes ($1)

2 cups shredded mild cheddar
  cheese ($1.25)

Preheat the oven to 350 degrees. Grease a 9 × 13-inch glass baking dish with non-stick cooking spray.

Add the leftover spaghetti sauce to the bottom of the prepared baking dish.

Spread the mixed vegetables over the sauce. Top with the leftover mashed potatoes and sprinkle the cheese over the top.

Bake in the preheated oven for 25 to 30 minutes until bubbly and cheese has melted and begun to turn golden. Let cool slightly before cutting and serving.

Serve Ten-Minute Shepherd's Pie.

Makes 4 servings

Cost $4.55

FRUGAL FACT: *You can freeze both leftover spaghetti sauce and leftover mashed potatoes. When you find you have each in your freezer, make this quick meal to use up those frozen leftovers. Assemble this dish with leftovers in just 10 minutes.*

FREEZER FRIENDLY

Beef Fajita Potpie

¾ pound ground beef, browned ($1.12)

1 can (10 ounces) diced tomatoes with green chilies, well drained ($.50)

1 bag (12 ounces) frozen pepper and onion blend ($.80)

2 tablespoons fajita seasoning ($.20)

1 tablespoon lime juice ($.05)

1 cup shredded Monterey Jack cheese ($.67)

1 store-bought or Homemade Pie Crust (page 267) ($.75)

Sour cream for serving ($.10)

Preheat the oven to 400 degrees. Grease a 9-inch glass pie plate with nonstick cooking spray.

In a large mixing bowl, toss together the browned ground beef, diced tomatoes with green chilies, pepper and onion blend, fajita seasoning, and lime juice. Pour into the prepared pie plate and top with the shredded cheese.

Place the pie crust over the beef mixture and cheese and press around the edges of the pie plate to seal. Make 4 to 6 decorative slits in the top of the crust to allow the steam to escape.

Bake in the preheated oven for 35 to 40 minutes until the crust begins to turn golden on top. Let cool slightly before serving.

Serve Beef Fajita Potpie with a dollop of sour cream for each serving.

Makes 4 servings

Cost $4.19

FRUGAL FACT: *You can substitute the same amount of taco seasoning for the fajita seasoning if you don't have any fajita seasoning on hand.*

FREEZER FRIENDLY

Cheeseburger Potpie

1 pound ground beef, browned ($1.49)

3 pickles, chopped ($.25)

1 small yellow onion, chopped ($.20)

1 can (15 ounces) diced tomatoes,
well drained ($.20)

2 tablespoons spicy mustard ($.10)

2 tablespoons ketchup ($.10)

1 cup shredded cheddar cheese ($.67)

1 store-bought or Homemade Pie
Crust (page 267) ($.75)

Fresh fruit, such as apple or orange slices ($.50)

Preheat the oven to 400 degrees. Grease a 9-inch glass pie plate with nonstick cooking spray.

Mix together the browned ground beef, pickles, onion, diced tomatoes, mustard, and ketchup in the pie plate. Sprinkle the cheese over the top of the meat mixture.

Lay the pie crust over the top and press along the edges of the pie plate to seal. Make 4 to 6 decorative slits in the top of the pie crust for the steam to escape.

Bake in the preheated oven for 35 to 40 minutes until the crust begins to turn golden. Let cool slightly before cutting and serving.

Serve Cheeseburger Potpie with fresh fruit as a side dish.

Makes 4 servings

Cost $4.26

FRUGAL FACT: *This is a simple recipe to double up and freeze. Place the doubled portion in a disposable pie pan and assemble as if you were going to bake it. Then freeze, and later defrost in the fridge before baking as directed in this recipe.*

FREEZER FRIENDLY

Ginger Beef and Broccoli Bake

1 pound stew beef ($2.49)

2 cups fresh broccoli florets ($.99)

1½ cups brown rice ($.60)

⅓ cup soy sauce ($.20)

4 cups hot water

1 teaspoon ground ginger ($.05)

½ teaspoon garlic salt ($.02)

½ teaspoon pepper

Preheat the oven to 350 degrees. Grease a 9 × 13-inch glass baking dish with non-stick cooking spray.

To the prepared baking dish, add the stew beef, broccoli florets, and rice and toss together. Pour the soy sauce and the water over the beef, broccoli, and rice. Sprinkle the ginger, garlic salt, and pepper over the mixture. Cover the baking dish tightly with aluminum foil.

Bake in the preheated oven for 1 hour and 15 minutes. Uncover and toss with a fork before serving.

If using white rice, decrease the cooking time to 50 to 55 minutes.

Serve Ginger Beef and Broccoli Bake.

Makes 4 servings

Cost $4.35

FRUGAL FACT: *Look for marked down packages of stew beef, as it can often be found for less than $2.49 per pound as part of a reduced-for-quick-sale promotion.*

Spinach Meatball Subs

¾ pound ground beef ($1.12)

1 cup bread crumbs ($.25)

1 egg ($.10)

1 teaspoon dried Italian seasoning ($.05)

1 box (10 ounces) frozen chopped spinach, cooked and well drained ($.50)

1 can (15 ounces) crushed tomatoes ($.20)

A few dashes of dried Italian seasoning, salt, and pepper ($.02)

4 sub sandwich rolls ($1.49)

4 slices provolone cheese ($.75)

Fresh fruit, such as apple slices or orange wedges ($.50)

Preheat the oven to 350 degrees. Grease an 8 × 8-inch glass baking dish with nonstick cooking spray.

In a mixing bowl, combine the ground beef, bread crumbs, egg, Italian seasoning, and cooked and drained spinach. Form sixteen 1½-inch meatballs and place into the prepared baking dish. Pour the crushed tomatoes over the top of the meatballs and sprinkle with a few dashes of Italian seasoning, salt, and pepper.

Bake in the preheated oven for 30 minutes, or until the meatballs have cooked through.

Slice open the sub sandwich rolls lengthwise and place 4 meatballs with some sauce onto each roll. Tear the cheese slices in half and place them over the meatballs. The heat from the meatballs and sauce will help the cheese to melt, or you can microwave the sub for 30 seconds to 1 minute, to melt the cheese completely.

Serve Spinach Meatball Subs with fresh fruit.

Makes 4 servings

Cost $4.98

FRUGAL FACT: *Prepare the meatballs ahead of time and flash freeze them to save a few minutes in preparing this dinner or for the Slow Cooker Spaghetti and Meatballs Florentine (page 75). If using premade frozen meatballs, bake them for 45 minutes to 1 hour, instead of 30 minutes as indicated in the recipe.*

Meat-and-Potatoes Casserole

1 pound ground beef, browned ($1.49)

1 small yellow onion, chopped ($.20)

4 carrots, peeled and diced ($.40)

1 can (15 ounces) diced tomatoes, with their juices ($.20)

1 teaspoon dried Italian seasoning ($.05)

1 teaspoon garlic powder ($.05)

6 medium Idaho potatoes, peeled and diced ($.80)

2 cups shredded cheddar cheese ($1.25)

Preheat the oven to 350 degrees. Grease a 9 × 13-inch glass baking dish with nonstick cooking spray.

In the prepared baking dish, gently toss the browned ground beef, onion, carrots, diced tomatoes, Italian seasoning, garlic powder, and potatoes until well combined. Sprinkle the shredded cheese over the top.

Cover with the dish with aluminum foil.

Bake in the preheated oven for 45 to 50 minutes until the potatoes are tender.

Serve Meat-and-Potatoes Casserole.

Makes 4 servings

Cost $4.44

FRUGAL FACT: *The perfect low-cost dinner for those husbands who prefer "meat-and-potato" meals only.*

Spanish Rice Casserole

1 pound ground beef, browned ($1.49)

1¼ cups white rice ($.25)

1 can (15 ounces) diced tomatoes with roasted garlic ($.20)

1 bag (12 ounces) frozen fiesta-style vegetables ($.80)

1¾ cups hot water

Salt and pepper

2 cups shredded mild cheddar cheese ($1.25)

Preheat the oven to 350 degrees. Grease a 9×13-inch glass baking dish with nonstick cooking spray.

To the prepared baking dish, add the browned ground beef, rice, diced tomatoes, vegetables, and the hot water. Season with salt and pepper to taste. Cover tightly with aluminum foil.

Bake in the preheated oven for 1 hour, or until the rice is tender. Uncover and sprinkle the shredded cheese over the top and return to the oven for 10 minutes more, or until the cheese has melted. Let cool slightly before serving.

Serve Spanish Rice Casserole.

Makes 4 servings

Cost $3.99

FRUGAL FACT: *If using brown rice, increase the cooking time to 1 hour and 15 minutes.*

Old-Fashioned Beef Stew

....

1 tablespoon extra-virgin olive
   oil ($.05)

¾ pound beef stew meat ($1.49)

1 teaspoon onion powder ($.05)

1 teaspoon garlic powder ($.05)

8 small red potatoes, quartered ($1.60)

6 carrots, peeled and cut into
   thirds ($.60)

1 can (15 ounces) diced tomatoes,
   with their juices ($.20)

2 cups hot water

1 teaspoon chopped parsley ($.05)

Salt and pepper

In a large pot or Dutch oven over medium-high heat, warm the olive oil. Add the beef stew meat and brown on all sides. Season with the onion powder, garlic powder, and salt and pepper to taste.

Once the beef has browned, add the potatoes, carrots, and diced tomatoes. Pour in the water and stir all of the ingredients together. Cover, reduce the heat to low, and simmer for 20 to 30 minutes.

If you wish to simmer it longer, then watch the liquid level and add more broth or water as needed. Let cool slightly before serving. Taste and adjust the seasoning with additional salt and pepper, if needed. Sprinkle with the chopped parsley.

Serve Old-Fashioned Beef Stew.

Makes 4 servings

Cost $4.09

FRUGAL FACT: *If you purchase a large beef roast on sale or special, cut off ¾ to 1 pound of meat and slice it into stew meat pieces. Store in the refrigerator to use later in the week, or label and freeze to use in future meals.*

MAKE-AHEAD MEAL

Pot Roast with Dilled Carrots and Potatoes

1 tablespoon extra-virgin olive oil ($.05)

1 tablespoon lemon juice ($.05)

1¼-pound chuck roast ($3.11)

½ cup water

Salt and pepper

4 small Idaho potatoes, peeled and cut into chunks ($.60)

1 pound baby carrots ($1)

1 teaspoon dill ($.10)

1 teaspoon garlic salt ($.05)

In a large pot or Dutch oven over high heat, warm the olive oil and lemon juice, add the chuck roast and sear all the sides. When the roast is seared, add the water, and season with salt and pepper.

Add the potato chunks and baby carrots around and on top of the roast in the pot. Sprinkle with the dill and garlic salt. Cover and cook over medium heat for 1 hour, or until the beef has cooked through. The cooking time may vary depending on the thickness of the roast.

Serve Pot Roast with Dilled Carrots and Potatoes.

Makes 4 servings

Cost $4.96

FRUGAL FACT: *The "never-pay-more-than" price for chuck roast is $2.49 per pound.*

SLOW COOKER ADAPTABLE

MAKE-AHEAD MEAL

Lemony Pasta with Ham and Peas, *page 67*

Lentil Curry with Chickpeas, Carrots, and Spinach, *page 225*

Skillet Taco Pie, *page 136*

Thai Chicken with Noodles, *page 93*

Sesame Shrimp and Pepper Stir Fry, *page 178*

Loaded Potato Frittata, *page 161*

Skillet Lasagna Florentine, *page 126*

One-Bowl Mocha Brownies, *page 250*

Beef Stew Biscuit Bake

1 tablespoon extra-virgin olive
  oil ($.05)
¾ pound beef stew meat ($1.49)
2 garlic cloves, crushed ($.05)
1 small yellow onion, diced ($.20)
4 carrots, peeled and chopped
  ($.40)

1 can (15 ounces) diced tomatoes,
  with their juices ($.20)
1 can (8 ounces) tomato sauce ($.33)
1 teaspoon dried Italian
  seasoning ($.05)
1 cup shredded mozzarella cheese
  ($.67)

BISCUIT TOPPING

2 cups all-purpose flour ($.40)
1 tablespoon sugar ($.01)
1 tablespoon baking powder ($.15)
1 teaspoon salt

½ teaspoon garlic powder ($.03)
4 tablespoons butter, melted ($.40)
1 cup milk ($.10)

Preheat the oven to 350 degrees.

In a large ovenproof pot or Dutch oven over medium-high heat, warm the olive oil and then brown the stew meat. Stir in the garlic cloves, onion, carrots, diced tomatoes, tomato sauce, and Italian seasoning. Season with a little salt and pepper. Reduce the heat to medium-low and cook for 8 to 10 minutes.

In a mixing bowl, whisk together the flour, sugar, baking powder, salt, and garlic powder. Then whisk in the melted butter and milk.

When the batter is mixed, sprinkle the shredded cheese over the bubbling stew and then pour the biscuit batter over the top. Transfer the pot or Dutch oven to the preheated oven and bake for 20 to 24 minutes until the biscuit crust has baked through and begun to turn golden on top.

Using heavy-duty oven mitts, carefully remove the pot or Dutch oven from the oven. Let cool slightly before serving.

Serve Beef Stew Biscuit Bake.

Makes 4 servings

Cost $4.53

FRUGAL FACT: *If you make biscuits or cornbread frequently, set up an assembly line and place all the dry ingredients into plastic bags and label them with the wet ingredients that will need to be mixed in to make the biscuits or cornbread.*

FREEZER FRIENDLY

Chili-Corn Tot Bake

1 pound ground beef ($1.49)

2 cups cooked red kidney beans ($.40)

1 can (15 ounces) diced tomatoes, with their juices ($.20)

1 can (8 ounces) tomato sauce ($.33)

2 teaspoons chili powder ($.10)

1 teaspoon minced onion ($.05)

1 can (15 ounces) corn kernels, drained ($.50)

1 pound Tater Tots ($1.04)

1 cup shredded sharp cheddar cheese ($.67)

Preheat the oven to 350 degrees.

In a large ovenproof pot or Dutch oven over medium-high heat, brown the ground beef. Drain and return it to the pot.

Stir in the beans, diced tomatoes, tomato sauce, chili powder, onion, and corn. Reduce the heat to low and let simmer for 10 minutes to allow the flavors to mingle.

Arrange the Tater Tots on top of the chili in the pot, then sprinkle the shredded cheese over the top. Transfer the pot to the preheated oven and bake for 20 to 25 minutes until the Tater Tots are cooked through and the cheese has melted.

Serve Chili-Corn Tot Bake.

Makes 4 servings

Cost $4.78 (Note: The cost will change with the substitution of canned beans.)

FRUGAL FACT: *My "never-pay-more-than" price for Tater Tots is $1 per pound.*

Dinnertime Chili Cheese Nachos

1 pound ground beef ($1.49)

1 small yellow onion, chopped ($.20)

1 can (15 ounces) diced tomatoes, with their juices ($.20)

1 can (8 ounces) tomato sauce ($.33)

2 small zucchini, about 1 pound, diced ($.79)

1 tablespoon chili powder ($.15)

1 teaspoon ground cumin ($.05)

Salt and pepper

4 to 6 cups corn tortilla chips ($1)

1 cup shredded cheddar cheese ($.67)

In a large pot or Dutch oven over medium-high heat, brown the ground beef with the onion. Drain and return the mixture to the pot.

Reduce the heat to low, and add the diced tomatoes, tomato sauce, zucchini, chili powder, and cumin. Season with salt and pepper to taste. Let the chili simmer for 5 to 10 minutes.

Place the tortilla chips on serving plates and top with the chili, then sprinkle with the shredded cheese. Microwave to melt the cheese, if the hot chili doesn't melt it first.

Serve Dinnertime Chili Cheese Nachos.

Makes 4 servings

Cost $4.88

FRUGAL FACT: *My "never-pay-more-than" price for a large bag of tortilla chips is $2. These store well in the pantry and are on sale during the summer and around the time of the Super Bowl.*

Balsamic Pot Roast with Pearl Onions

1 pound chuck roast ($2.49)

Salt and pepper

4 medium Idaho potatoes, peeled and cut into chunks ($.60)

4 carrots, peeled and cut into -inch pieces ($.40)

1 bag (12 ounces) frozen pearl onions ($.88)

1 teaspoon dried Italian seasoning ($.05)

¼ cup balsamic vinegar ($.25)

Add the chuck roast to the insert of a 5-quart or larger slow cooker. Sprinkle with salt and pepper.

Add the potato, carrots, and pearl onions around and over the top of the chuck roast. Sprinkle the Italian seasoning over all the ingredients, then slowly drizzle the balsamic vinegar over all the ingredients. Season with additional salt and pepper, if needed.

Set the slow cooker on low and cook for 8 hours. When cooked, transfer the roast, potatoes, carrots, and onions from the slow cooker to a serving platter. Let the roast cool slightly before slicing and serving.

Serve Balsamic Pot Roast with Pearl Onions.

Makes 4 servings

Cost $4.67

FRUGAL FACT: *If more economical you can purchase a larger roast and then cut it into 1-pound portions to use in recipes like this. The other roast portion could also be cut into chunks and used in soup, or roasted and then shredded for shredded beef sandwiches.*

MAKE-AHEAD MEAL

Slow Cooker Beef Roast with Red Potatoes and Butternut Squash

....

4 red potatoes, quartered ($.80)

1 small butternut squash, about 1 pound, peeled and cubed ($.89)

1¼ pounds beef chuck roast ($3.11)

1 teaspoon garlic powder ($.05)

1 teaspoon onion powder ($.05)

Salt and pepper

Place the potatoes and butternut squash in the insert of a 5-quart or larger slow cooker. Place the beef chuck roast on top and sprinkle with the garlic powder, onion powder, and salt and pepper.

Set the slow cooker on low and cook for 8 hours.

Let the beef roast cool slightly before slicing and serving.

Serve Slow Cooker Beef Roast with Red Potatoes and Butternut Squash.

Makes 4 servings

Cost $4.90

FRUGAL FACT: *The perfect make-ahead slow cooker meal—simply place all the ingredients into a gallon-size plastic freezer bag and freeze for when you need a quick "dump-and-go" slow cooker meal. Let thaw in the fridge overnight before placing in the slow cooker in the morning.*

MAKE-AHEAD MEAL

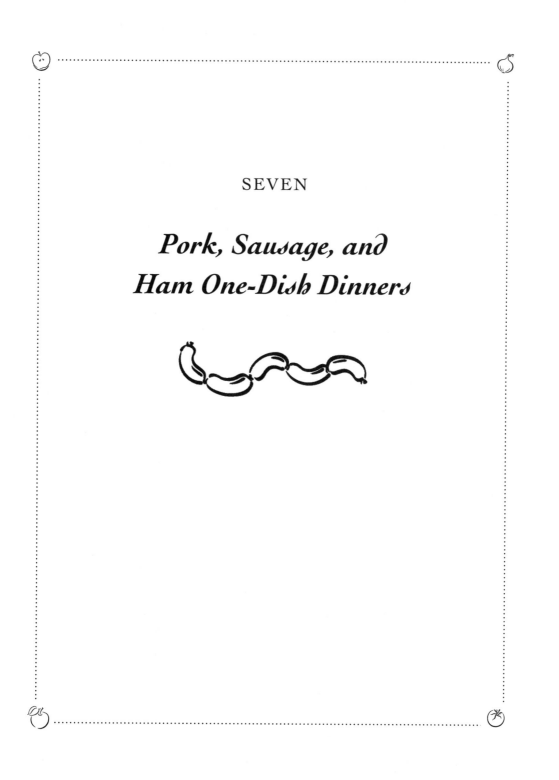

SEVEN

Pork, Sausage, and Ham One-Dish Dinners

Sausage, Potato, and Pepper Skillet

....

1 tablespoon extra-virgin olive
   oil ($.05)

1 small yellow onion, diced ($.20)

4 Idaho potatoes, peeled and diced
   into ¾-inch pieces ($.60)

1 pound mild Italian sausage links,
   casings removed, sliced into 1-inch
   pieces ($2.99)

1 can (15 ounces) diced tomatoes,
   with their juices ($.20)

1 teaspoon dried oregano ($.05)

1 green bell pepper, seeded and
   diced ($.59)

Garlic salt

Black pepper

In a large 12-inch skillet or sauté pan over medium-high heat, warm the olive oil. Add the onion and potatoes and sauté for 2 to 3 minutes. Add about ½ cup of water and continue to cook the potatoes for another 3 to 4 minutes. Add the sliced sausage, diced tomatoes, and the oregano. Cover tightly with a lid and cook for 10 to 15 minutes until the sausage has cooked through.

Add the bell pepper and remove the skillet from the heat; the bell pepper will cook with the heat from other ingredients. Season with garlic salt and pepper to taste.

Serve Sausage, Potato, and Pepper Skillet.

Makes 4 servings

Cost $4.68

FRUGAL FACT: *Cut the casings of the sausage lengthwise and remove the sausage meat. Then using kitchen shears, cut the sausage into 1-inch-wide slices.*

Sausage "Brinner" Skillet

1 pound ground breakfast sausage ($2)

1 small yellow onion, chopped ($.20)

8 eggs ($.80)

1 can (15 ounces) diced tomatoes, drained ($.20)

1 small zucchini, about ⅔ pound, chopped ($.50)

1 cup shredded mild cheddar cheese ($.67)

Fresh fruit, such as pineapple slices or orange wedges ($.50)

In a 12-inch cast-iron skillet over medium-high heat, brown the breakfast sausage with the onion.

When the meat has browned and cooked through, reduce the heat to medium. Whisk in the 8 eggs, and scramble the eggs with the sausage. Once the eggs have cooked, stir in the diced tomatoes and zucchini and cook 2 to 3 minutes more, then top with the shredded cheese.

Remove from the heat and let the cheese melt over the top. Serve immediately.

Serve Sausage "Brinner" Skillet with fresh fruit as a side dish.

Makes 4 servings

Cost $4.87

FRUGAL FACT: *Wrap any leftover sausage and eggs in tortillas for a quick breakfast burrito the next morning.*

FREEZER FRIENDLY

Breakfast Potpie

1 tablespoon extra-virgin olive
   oil ($.05)
8 eggs ($.80)
2 garlic cloves, crushed ($.05)
Salt and pepper
1 bag (12 ounces) frozen cut
   broccoli ($.80)

1 cup diced leftover ham ($1)
¼ cup milk ($.03)
1 cup shredded cheddar cheese ($.67)
1 store-bought or Homemade Pie
   Crust (page 267) ($.75)

Preheat the oven to 375 degrees.

In a 12-inch ovenproof skillet or sauté pan over medium-high heat, warm the olive oil. Scramble the eggs with the garlic and salt and pepper to taste. Add the broccoli and ham and warm with the eggs for 2 to 3 minutes. Remove from the heat and pour the milk into the bottom of the skillet.

Sprinkle the shredded cheese over the top and then place the pie crust on top and carefully press the crust around the edges of the skillet to seal. Make 4 to 6 decorative slits in the top to allow the steam to escape.

Bake the potpie in the preheated oven for 30 to 35 minutes until the crust begins to turn golden.

Using heavy-duty oven mitts, remove the skillet from the oven carefully as the handle will be very hot. Let cool slightly before serving.

Serve Breakfast Potpie.

Makes 4 servings

Cost $4.15

FRUGAL FACT: *Schedule breakfast for dinner at least twice a month, or even once a week. It is generally a simple and frugal way to keep your family and pocketbook full.*

Sweet-and-Spicy Sausage Cornbread Skillet Bake

....

1 pound all-natural ground pork
    sausage ($2)
1 can (15 ounces) corn kernels,
    drained ($.50)

1 can (10 ounces) diced tomatoes
    with green chilies, drained ($.20)
1 cup shredded Monterey Jack cheese
    ($.67)

CORNBREAD TOPPING

1 cup all-purpose flour ($.20)
1 cup yellow cornmeal ($.35)
¾ cup sugar ($.08)
2 teaspoons baking powder ($.10)
1 teaspoon salt
1 egg ($.10)

1 cup milk ($.10)
¼ cup canola or vegetable oil ($.10)
2 tablespoons honey ($.05)
2 tablespoons sugar, for
    sprinkling ($.02)

Preheat the oven to 400 degrees.

In a 12-inch cast-iron skillet over medium-high heat, brown the all-natural pork sausage. Drain and return to the skillet. Then add the corn and diced tomatoes with green chilies. Continue to cook over medium-high heat until most of the liquid has evaporated from the skillet; 3 to 5 minutes depending on how much liquid needs to cook off. Sprinkle the shredded cheese over the sausage mixture and cook for 1 to 2 minutes more until most of the cheese has melted.

In a medium mixing bowl, whisk together the flour, cornmeal, sugar, baking powder, and salt. Add the egg, milk, oil, and honey and whisk until a smooth batter forms, about 2 minutes.

Pour the cornbread batter over the top of the cheese in the skillet and let cook for about 2 minutes, or until the cornbread batter begins to set along the edges of the skillet.

Transfer the skillet to the preheated oven and bake for 18 to 20 minutes until the cornbread has baked through and begun to turn golden on top. Using heavy-duty oven mitts, remove the skillet from oven carefully as the handle will be very hot. Let cool slightly before serving.

Serve Sweet-and-Spicy Sausage Cornbread Skillet Bake.

Makes 4 servings

Cost $4.47

FRUGAL FACT: *Turn this into an inexpensive gluten-free meal by substituting 1 cup of brown rice flour for the 1 cup of all-purpose flour in the cornbread mix.*

FREEZER FRIENDLY

Loaded Potato Frittata

6 slices turkey bacon or all-natural
   bacon ($.75)
4 medium Idaho potatoes, peeled and
   diced ($.60)
8 eggs ($.80)
½ cup milk ($.05)
¼ cup sour cream ($.25)
Salt and pepper
1½ cups shredded cheddar
   cheese ($.94)
1 bunch scallions, sliced ($.50)

Fresh fruit, such as clementines, apple slices, bananas, or cantaloupe wedges
   ($.50)

Preheat the oven to 350 degrees.

Cook the bacon in a 12-inch cast-iron skillet over medium to medium-low heat. Transfer the bacon to paper towels to drain, and then crumble. Reserve the bacon fat in the skillet.

In the same skillet, sauté the potatoes in the bacon fat over medium-high heat for 5 to 7 minutes until they begin to soften. Once softened, return the crumbled bacon to the skillet and combine with the potatoes.

In a mixing bowl, whisk together the eggs, milk, and sour cream. Season with a little salt and pepper. Pour the egg mixture over the softened potatoes and cook over medium-low heat for about 3 minutes, or until you see the eggs along the edges begin to set.

Transfer the skillet to the preheated oven and bake for 15 to 20 minutes until the eggs in the middle have set. Sprinkle the shredded cheese over the top and then bake for 5 minutes more.

Once the cheese has melted, carefully remove the skillet from the oven. Be sure to use heavy-duty oven mitts as the handle will be hot. Let cool slightly before slicing.

Serve Loaded Potato Frittata garnished with sliced scallions and with a side of fresh fruit.

Makes 4 servings

Cost $4.39

FRUGAL FACT: *My "never-pay-more-than" price for a package of turkey bacon or all-natural bacon is $2. They often go on sale for close to that price, and every few months coupons are released in the newspaper and online.*

Pepper Pork Tacos

....

1 pound leftover shredded pork ($1.99)

1 bag (12 ounces) frozen pepper and onion blend ($.80)

1 tablespoon Homemade Taco Seasoning (page 266) ($.10)

1 cup shredded iceberg lettuce ($.25)

1 cup shredded Monterey Jack cheese ($.64)

¼ cup sour cream ($.25)

8 hard taco shells ($.75)

In a large 12-inch skillet or sauté pan over medium-high heat, sauté the shredded pork with the pepper and onion blend and the taco seasoning for 5 to 7 minutes until the vegetables have defrosted and the meat is cooked through.

Stuff the individual taco shells with the pork and pepper mixture, shredded lettuce, shredded cheese, and a dollop of sour cream.

Serve Pepper Pork Tacos.

Makes 8 tacos

Cost $4.78

FRUGAL FACT: *When you see pork roast or pork tenderloins on sale for $1.99 per pound or less, purchase a roast that can be used for 2 or 3 meals. When writing your meal plan, have the roast one day, then plan to use the leftover shredded pork for these tacos or with some BBQ sauce as sandwiches later in the week. The leftover shredded pork can also be frozen for use in a future meal.*

Pork Chop Apple Stuffing Bake

....

4 pork chops, about 1¼ pounds ($2)

1 package (8 ounces) sage stuffing mix ($1.19)

2 Golden Delicious apples, cored, and chopped ($.50)

2 celery stalks, chopped ($.20)

1 cup raisins ($.75)

2 cups hot water

Salt and pepper

Preheat the oven to 350 degrees. Grease a 9 × 13-inch baking dish with non-stick cooking spray.

Place the pork chops into the bottom of the prepared baking dish.

In a mixing bowl, toss together the stuffing mix, apples, celery, and raisins. Pour the hot water over the mixture and toss until the stuffing has absorbed the water. Season to taste with salt and pepper.

Spread the stuffing mixture over the top of the pork chops, covering the pork chops completely. Cover the baking dish with aluminum foil.

Bake in the preheated oven for 30 minutes. Remove the foil and bake for 20 to 25 minutes more until the pork chops have cooked through. The cooking time may vary depending on the thickness of the pork chops.

Serve Pork Chop Apple Stuffing Bake.

Makes 4 servings

Cost $4.64

FRUGAL FACT: *Make Homemade Stuffing (page 269) for a fraction of the cost of store-bought, and use 4 cups of the stuffing for this recipe.*

Ginger Pork Chop Casserole

3 sweet potatoes, about 1½ pounds, peeled and thinly sliced ($.74)

Juice of 1 orange ($.33)

4 boneless pork chops, about 1¼ pounds ($2.48)

½ teaspoon garlic powder ($.03)

1 teaspoon ground ginger ($.05)

1 small yellow onion, diced ($.20)

Salt and pepper

Preheat the oven to 350 degrees. Grease a 9 × 13-inch glass baking dish with nonstick cooking spray.

Spread out the sweet potato slices evenly in the bottom of the prepared baking dish. Sprinkle with a few dashes of the ginger.

Place the pork chops on top of the sweet potato layer and season with the garlic powder, ginger, and salt and pepper. Cover the baking dish with aluminum foil.

Bake in the preheated oven for 30 minutes, then uncover and bake for 25 minutes more, or until the pork chops have cooked through and the sweet potatoes are tender.

Serve Ginger Pork Chop Casserole.

Makes 4 servings

Cost $3.83

FRUGAL FACT: *My "never-pay-more-than" price for boneless pork chops is $1.99 per pound.*

Smothered Italian Pork Chops

4 bone-in pork chops, about 1½ pounds ($2.25)

Salt and pepper

1 small yellow onion, chopped ($.20)

4 celery stalks, chopped ($.40)

4 small potatoes, peeled and diced into ½-inch pieces ($.60)

½ cup store-bought or Homemade Basic Vinaigrette (page 261) ($.25)

1 teaspoon dried Italian seasoning ($.05)

Preheat the oven to 350 degrees. Grease a 9×13-inch baking dish with nonstick cooking spray.

Place the pork chops in the bottom of the prepared baking dish and sprinkle each side with a little salt and pepper.

In a mixing bowl, toss together the onion, celery, potatoes, basic vinaigrette dressing, and Italian seasoning. Pour the mixture over the top of the pork chops in the baking dish and spread it out evenly. Sprinkle a little salt and pepper over the top.

Bake, uncovered, in the preheated oven for 45 to 50 minutes until the pork chops are no longer pink in the middle.

Serve Smothered Italian Pork Chops.

Makes 4 servings

Cost $3.75

FRUGAL FACT: *Look for larger packages of bone-in pork chops that are marked down for quick sale. Double this recipe and use the larger package of pork chops when you have company coming for dinner. A simple recipe that is sure to impress!*

MAKE-AHEAD MEAL

Cornbread Pork Chop Casserole

....

4 bone-in pork chops, about
   1¼ pounds ($2.24)
½ teaspoon garlic powder ($.03)
Salt and pepper
2 Granny Smith apples, cored and
   thinly sliced ($.50)

1 bag (14 ounces) cornbread stuffing
   mix ($1.49)
1 small yellow onion, chopped
   ($.20)
1¾ cups hot water

Preheat the oven to 350 degrees. Grease a 2-quart casserole or a 7 × 11-inch glass baking dish with nonstick cooking spray.

Arrange the pork chops in the bottom of the casserole or baking dish. Sprinkle each side with garlic powder and salt and pepper. Arrange the apple slices on top of the pork chops.

In a mixing bowl, combine the cornbread stuffing mix and chopped onions. Toss with the hot water. Spread the moist cornbread mixture over the pork chops and apples. Cover the baking dish tightly with aluminum foil.

Bake in the preheated oven for 25 minutes. Then remove the foil and bake, uncovered, for 10 to 15 minutes more until the pork chops have cooked through. The cooking time may vary depending on the thickness of the pork chops. Let cool slightly before serving. Season with additional salt and pepper to taste, if needed.

Serve Cornbread Pork Chop Casserole.

Makes 4 servings

Cost $4.46

FRUGAL FACT: *The "stock-up-now-price" for bone-in pork chops is $1.49 per pound. And don't forget to grab a few extra bags of stuffing mix during the sales in November and December.*

Ham, Potato, and Asparagus Bake

1 pound fresh asparagus, woody stem
   ends snapped off and discarded, cut
   into 1-inch pieces ($.99)
½ pound ham, diced ($1.99)
2 medium Idaho potatoes, peeled
   and cut into ¼-inch pieces ($.30)

8 eggs ($.80)
½ cup milk ($.02)
1 teaspoon paprika ($.10)
Black pepper
¼ cup grated Parmesan cheese ($.25)

2 bananas, cut in half ($.40)

Preheat the oven to 350 degrees. Grease a 9 × 13-inch glass baking dish with nonstick cooking spray.

In the prepared baking dish, toss together the asparagus, ham, and potato.

In a mixing bowl, whisk together the eggs, milk, paprika, and a couple of dashes of pepper. Pour over the asparagus, ham, and potato in the baking dish. Cover tightly with aluminum foil.

Bake in the preheated oven for 40 minutes. After 40 minutes, remove the foil and bake, uncovered, for 5 to 10 minutes more until the eggs have turned golden brown on top.

Remove from oven and let cool slightly before serving. Sprinkle 1 tablespoon of the grated Parmesan cheese on each serving.

Serve Ham, Potato, and Asparagus Bake with fresh bananas.

Makes 4 servings

Cost $4.85

FRUGAL FACT: *Look for specials on ham during the Easter holiday and Christmas holiday seasons. Buy more than you need for your holiday feast and then cut up and freeze the leftover ham for future meals.*

Spinach, Ham, and Potato Gratin

4 tablespoons butter ($.40)

4 small Idaho potatoes, thinly sliced, divided ($.60)

2 tablespoons all-purpose flour ($.02)

1½ cups milk ($.15)

Salt and pepper

4 slices provolone or Swiss cheese ($.75)

8 ounces fresh spinach leaves ($1)

4 ounces sliced ham deli meat ($1)

3 tablespoons sour cream ($.18)

½ teaspoon salt

Black pepper

Fresh fruit, such as apple slices or orange slices ($.50)

Preheat the oven to 350 degrees.

While the oven is preheating, put the butter into a 9 × 13-inch glass baking dish and place it in the preheating oven to melt.

Meanwhile, slice the potatoes with a mandoline or sharp knife. The potato slices shouldn't be more than ⅛ inch thick.

Once the butter has melted, remove the baking dish from the oven, whisk in the flour and then 1 cup of the milk. Place half of the thinly sliced potatoes into the sauce in the baking dish. Season with salt and pepper to taste. Place the 4 slices of cheese over the potatoes, then top with the spinach leaves.

Place the sliced ham over the spinach leaves, covering the entire dish. Place the remaining sliced potatoes over the top.

In a 2-cup liquid measuring container, whisk the sour cream with the remaining ½ cup of milk and the ½ teaspoon salt. Pour the sour cream–milk mixture over the potatoes in the baking dish. Sprinkle pepper over the top and cover tightly with aluminum foil.

Bake in the preheated oven for 40 to 45 minutes. Let cool slightly before slicing and serving.

Serve Spinach, Ham, and Potato Gratin with a side of fresh fruit.

Makes 4 servings

Cost $4.60

FRUGAL FACT: *Substitute 2 cups of leftover diced holiday ham for the sliced ham deli meat.*

Baked Potato Casserole

8 medium Idaho potatoes ($1.20)
¼ cup butter ($.40)
½ cup sour cream ($.50)
1 cup leftover diced ham ($1)
1 bag (12 ounces) frozen broccoli
   florets ($.80)

Salt and pepper
1 cup shredded cheddar cheese ($.63)
Chopped chives for garnish ($.10)

Preheat the oven to 400 degrees. Pierce each potato with a fork and bake in the preheated oven for 1 hour, or until soft.

Reduce the oven temperature to 350 degrees. Grease a 9 × 13-inch glass baking dish with nonstick cooking spray.

Once the potatoes have baked and are cool enough to handle, scoop out the flesh of each potato into a mixing bowl; do not mash. Toss with the butter, sour cream, ham, and broccoli florets. Season with salt and pepper to taste.

Place the potato mixture into the prepared baking dish. Sprinkle the cheese over the top. Bake for 25 to 30 minutes until the broccoli is tender and cheese begins to golden. Let cool slightly before serving.

Serve Baked Potato Casserole garnished with chopped chives.

Makes 4 servings

Cost $4.63

FRUGAL FACT: *Save the potato "shells" and pop them in the freezer. Turn them into a cheesy vegetable dish later by defrosting the shells, brushing with olive oil, adding mixed vegetables and cheese, and baking for 15 minutes at 350 degrees.*

Ham and Broccoli Breakfast "Brinner"

2 cups cooked and leftover ham ($2)

1 large head broccoli, cut into
florets ($.79)

2 slices whole wheat bread, torn ($.20)

6 eggs ($.60)

½ cup milk ($.05)

¼ cup Dijon mustard ($.20)

1 teaspoon garlic powder ($.05)

1 teaspoon black pepper

½ teaspoon paprika ($.05)

Fresh fruit, such as cantaloupe wedges or pineapple slices ($.50)

Preheat the oven to 350 degrees. Grease an 8×8-inch glass baking dish with nonstick cooking spray.

Gently toss the ham, broccoli florets, and torn bread pieces in the bottom of the prepared baking dish.

In a mixing bowl, whisk together the eggs, milk, Dijon mustard, garlic powder, and pepper. Pour over the ham, broccoli, and bread in the baking dish. Sprinkle the paprika over the top.

Bake, uncovered, in the preheated oven for 55 to 60 minutes until the eggs have cooked through and begun to turn golden on top.

Serve Ham and Broccoli Breakfast "Brinner" with fresh fruit.

Makes 4 servings

Cost $4.44

FRUGAL FACT: *Freeze leftover diced ham in 2-cup portions. It thaws quickly in the refrigerator or microwave and makes meal preparation easy and simple.*

Slow Cooker Pork Roast with Sweet Potatoes and Apples

....

1½-pound pork shoulder roast ($1.93)

4 small lunchbox-size apples, peeled, cored, and diced ($1)

3 medium sweet potatoes, about 1½ pounds, peeled and cubed ($.74)

½ cup apple juice ($.10)

Salt and pepper

Bread and butter ($.50)

Place the pork shoulder roast in the insert of a 5-quart or larger slow cooker. Place the apples around the pork and the sweet potatoes over the top of the apples and pork roast. Pour over the apple juice and season with salt and pepper.

Set the slow cooker on low and cook for 8 hours.

Serve Slow Cooker Pork Roast with Sweet Potatoes and Apples with bread and butter.

Makes 4 servings

Cost $4.27

FRUGAL FACT: *Sweet potatoes have a long shelf life and will keep on your countertop for up to 4 weeks after purchasing. When you see them on sale for $.49 per pound, or less, grab a few extras to use in the few weeks after buying them.*

MAKE-AHEAD MEAL

EIGHT

Fish and Seafood One-Dish Dinners

Creole Shrimp and Cornbread Skillet Bake

....

14 ounces tailless frozen uncooked
   shrimp ($2.99)
1 can (15 ounces) diced tomatoes,
   drained ($.20)
1 small zucchini, about ⅔ pound,
   chopped ($.50)

1 teaspoon garlic powder ($.05)
1 tablespoon minced onion ($.10)
2 teaspoons Creole seasoning ($.04)
Salt and pepper

CORNBREAD TOPPING

1 cup all-purpose flour ($.20)
1 cup yellow cornmeal ($.35)
¾ cup sugar ($.08)
2 teaspoons baking powder ($.10)
1 teaspoon salt

1 egg ($.10)
1 cup milk ($.10)
¼ cup canola or vegetable oil ($.10)
2 tablespoons honey ($.05)

Preheat the oven to 350 degrees.

In a large, ovenproof 12-inch skillet or sauté pan over medium-high heat, cook the shrimp with the tomatoes, zucchini, garlic powder, onion, Creole seasoning, and salt and pepper for 7 to 9 minutes.

In a mixing bowl, whisk together the flour, cornmeal, sugar, baking powder, and salt. Whisk in the egg, milk, oil, and honey. Pour the cornbread batter over the cooked shrimp and vegetables.

Transfer the skillet into the preheated oven and bake for 18 to 20 minutes until the cornbread has baked through in the middle.

Using heavy-duty oven mitts, carefully remove the skillet from the oven as the handle will be hot. Let cool slightly before serving.

Serve Creole Shrimp and Cornbread Skillet Bake.

Makes 4 servings

Cost $4.96

FRUGAL FACT: *This is a perfect example of a meal that pairs more expensive ingredients, like shrimp with other inexpensive ingredients. This helps to keep meal costs and overall grocery costs to a minimum. Another meal example would be salmon fillets, baked and paired with brown rice and steamed broccoli.*

FREEZER FRIENDLY

Sesame Shrimp and Pepper Stir-Fry

1 tablespoon extra-virgin olive
   oil ($.05)
1 teaspoon sesame oil ($.10)
14 ounces tailless frozen uncooked
   shrimp ($2.99)
1 bag (12 ounces) frozen pepper and
   onion blend ($.80)

1 teaspoon garlic powder ($.05)
Salt and pepper
1 cup white rice ($.20)
1 to 1¼ cups hot water
¼ cup toasted sesame seeds ($.50)

In a large 12-inch skillet or sauté pan over medium-high heat, warm the olive oil and sesame oil. Add the shrimp and sauté with the pepper and onion blend and cook for 6 to 8 minutes. Season with garlic powder and salt and pepper to taste.

Add the rice with hot water; the water should be deep enough to cover the rice. Stir and press the rice down into the liquid, then cover. Reduce the heat to low and cook for 18 to 20 minutes, or until the rice is tender. Stir once while the rice is cooking, quickly replacing the lid to keep the steam from escaping.

Once the rice is tender, remove the skillet from the heat and let cool slightly before serving. Sprinkle the toasted sesame seeds onto each serving.

Serve Sesame Shrimp and Pepper Stir-Fry.

Makes 4 servings

Cost $4.69

FRUGAL FACT: *Two cups of leftover rice will easily revive if tossed into the skillet after the shrimp and peppers have cooked down. Serve immediately sprinkled with the toasted sesame seeds.*

Creole Chicken and Shrimp Pilaf

1 tablespoon extra-virgin olive oil ($.05)

1 small chicken breast, about ⅓ pound, cut into bite-size pieces ($.62)

14 ounces tailless frozen uncooked shrimp ($2.99)

1 cup frozen chopped green bell pepper ($.40)

½ cup frozen chopped onion ($.20)

2 tablespoons Creole seasoning ($.25)

1 cup brown rice ($.40)

2½ cups hot water

Salt and pepper

In a large pot or Dutch oven over medium-high heat, warm the olive oil. Add the chicken pieces and sauté with the shrimp for 2 to 3 minutes.

Stir in the bell pepper and onions. Mix in the Creole seasoning and cook over high heat for 3 to 5 minutes more. Stir in the rice and the hot water and bring to a boil. Reduce the heat to medium, cover, and cook for 45 to 50 minutes until the rice is tender. Season with salt and pepper to taste.

If using white rice, reduce the cooking time to 15 to 20 minutes.

Serve Creole Chicken and Shrimp Pilaf.

Makes 4 servings

Cost $4.91

FRUGAL FACT: *Save a few extra minutes in the kitchen by buying the already de-veined and cooked shrimp with the tails removed.*

Broccoli, Tuna, and Rice Bake

2 cups fresh broccoli florets ($.99)

3 cans (6 ounces) tuna in water, drained ($1.50)

1½ cups white rice ($.30)

1 teaspoon garlic powder ($.05)

1 teaspoon onion powder ($.05)

½ teaspoon paprika ($.05)

½ teaspoon salt

½ teaspoon pepper

3½ cups hot water

2 cups shredded mozzarella cheese ($1.25)

¼ cup grated Parmesan cheese ($.25)

Preheat the oven to 350 degrees. Grease a 9 × 13-inch glass baking dish with non-stick cooking spray.

Add the broccoli florets to the prepared baking dish. Add the tuna and toss gently so that it is distributed throughout. Sprinkle the rice throughout the casserole, and then sprinkle the seasoning all over the top. Pour the hot water over the entire mixture. Cover the casserole tightly with aluminum foil.

Bake in the preheated oven for 45 minutes.

Remove the casserole from the oven, uncover, and toss the cooked rice, broccoli, and tuna with a fork. Sprinkle the shredded mozzarella cheese and the grated Parmesan cheese over the top of the casserole. Return the casserole to the oven, uncovered, and bake for another 10 to 15 minutes until the cheeses have melted and begun to turn golden on top.

Serve Broccoli, Tuna, and Rice Bake.

Makes 4 servings

Cost $4.44

FRUGAL FACT: *If you prefer to use frozen broccoli florets, reduce the amount of water that you add to the casserole to 3¼ cups. Using a 12-ounce bag of frozen broccoli florets could reduce the overall cost of the meal by $.75.*

FREEZER FRIENDLY

Tuna Quesadillas

2 cans (6 ounces) tuna in water, drained ($1)

1 red bell pepper, seeded and chopped ($1)

2 ounces cream cheese, softened ($.25)

2 cups shredded Colby-Jack cheese ($1.25)

8 soft taco-size flour tortillas ($1)

Fresh fruit, such as bananas, apple slices or cantaloupe wedges ($.50)

In a large mixing bowl, stir together the tuna, bell pepper, cream cheese, and shredded Colby-Jack cheese.

Lay a tortilla flat on a large electric griddle and top with ½ cup of the tuna mixture, then place another tortilla over the top. Press down with a large spatula, to help the top tortilla stick as the cheese melts. Cook for 1 to 2 minutes on each side. The quesadilla will cook quickly, so don't leave it unattended. Repeat the procedure to cook the other 3 quesadillas. Let cool slightly before cutting and serving.

Serve Tuna Quesadillas with fresh fruit.

Makes 4 quesadillas

Cost $5.00

FRUGAL FACT: *My "never-pay-more-than" price for a 6-ounce can of tuna is $.50. They go on sale regularly for that price, and can even be found for free if a coupon is in circulation at the same time as the sale.*

Spicy Tuna Noodle Casserole

12 ounces rotini pasta ($.37)

1 small yellow onion, chopped ($.20)

1 can (15 ounces) corn kernels, drained ($.50)

1 cup store-bought salsa or Homemade Salsa Fresca (page 260) ($.75)

½ cup sour cream ($.50)

3 pouches tuna in water, drained ($1.50)

1 cup shredded pepper jack cheese ($.67)

In a large pot or Dutch oven, cook the pasta as directed on the package. Drain and set aside.

In the same pot or Dutch oven, combine the onion, corn, salsa, sour cream, and tuna and cook for 3 to 5 minutes. Return the pasta to the pot and the stir in the shredded pepper jack cheese. Let the pasta sit in the pot on the warm burner for 2 to 3 minutes to allow the cheese to melt. Remove the pot from the heat once the cheese has melted. Let cool slightly before serving.

Serve Spicy Tuna Noodle Casserole.

Makes 4 servings

Cost $4.49 (Note: The cost will change with the substitution of store-bought salsa.)

FRUGAL FACT: *My "never-pay-more-than" price for the tuna pouches is the same as the 6-ounce cans of tuna, or $.50. And just like the canned tuna, they can also be found for free with the right coupon matchup.*

NINE

Chili, Stew, and Soup One-Dish Dinners

Zucchini Chicken Chili

1 tablespoon extra-virgin olive
   oil ($.05)
1 small yellow onion, chopped ($.20)
2 medium zucchini, about 1¼
   pounds, chopped ($.98)
6 boneless, skinless chicken thighs,
   about 1¼ lb., cut into 1-inch pieces
   ($2.49)
Salt and pepper

1 can (15 ounces) white beans,
   drained and rinsed ($.68)
1 cup store-bought or Homemade
   Chicken Stock (page 256) (free, if
   homemade)
1 cup hot water
¼ cup lime juice ($.10)
½ cup sour cream ($.50)

In a large pot or Dutch oven over medium-high heat, warm the olive oil, add the onion, zucchini, and chicken thigh pieces along with salt and pepper and sauté for 7 to 9 minutes until the chicken pieces have cooked through.

Stir in the white beans, chicken stock, hot water, and lime juice and bring to a boil. Reduce the heat to medium-low and simmer for 15 to 20 minutes.

Remove from the heat and stir in the sour cream just before serving.

Serve Zucchini Chicken Chili warm.

Makes 4 servings.

Cost $5.00 (Note: The cost will change with the substitution of store-bought chicken stock.)

FRUGAL FACT: *You can substitute about 1 pound of diced boneless, skinless chicken breast for the boneless chicken thighs if you don't have any chicken thighs on hand.*

SLOW COOKER ADAPTABLE

FREEZER FRIENDLY

Meat-and-Potatoes-Man Chili

1 pound ground beef ($1.49)

1 small yellow onion, chopped ($.20)

2 garlic cloves, crushed ($.05)

2 tablespoons chili powder ($.30)

1 can (15 ounces) tomato sauce ($.20)

1 can (15 ounces) diced tomatoes, with their juices ($.20)

1 can (15 ounces) red kidney beans, with their liquid ($.68)

4 small Idaho potatoes, peeled and diced ($.60)

1½ cups hot water

Salt and pepper

½ cup shredded cheddar cheese ($.32)

Sour cream for serving ($.10)

In a large pot or Dutch oven over medium-high heat, brown the ground beef with the onion and garlic. Stir in the chili powder and sauté for about 30 seconds. Drain and return the mixture to the pot.

Stir in the tomato sauce, diced tomatoes, kidney beans, potatoes and the hot water. Season with salt and pepper to taste and bring to a boil. Cover, reduce the heat to medium, and cook for 10 to 15 minutes until the potatoes are tender.

Serve Meat-and-Potatoes-Man Chili warm with a pinch of cheese and a dollop of sour cream in each serving bowl.

Makes 4 servings

Cost $4.14

FRUGAL FACT: *Fill your hungry husband's belly with this hearty chili, and without draining your grocery budget.*

Four-Bean Chili

....

1 tablespoon extra-virgin olive
   oil ($.05)

1 small red onion, chopped ($.40)

4 garlic cloves, crushed ($.10)

1 tablespoon chili powder ($.15)

1 can (15 ounces) diced tomatoes,
   with their juices ($.20)

1 can (15 ounces) crushed
   tomatoes ($.20)

1 can (15 ounces) black beans, rinsed
   and drained ($.68)

1 can (15 ounces) dark red kidney
   beans, rinsed and drained ($.68)

1 can (15 ounces) red kidney beans,
   rinsed and drained ($.68)

1 can (15 ounces) pinto beans, rinsed
   and drained ($.68)

½ teaspoon ground cumin ($.03)

½ teaspoon paprika ($.05)

Salt and pepper

Sour cream for serving ($.10)

In a large pot or Dutch oven over medium-high heat, warm the olive oil. Add the onion and garlic and sauté for 2 to 3 minutes. Stir in the chili powder and sauté for about 30 seconds.

Add the diced tomatoes and the crushed tomatoes. Then add the black beans, dark kidney beans, red kidney beans, and pinto beans. Stir in the cumin and the paprika and bring to a boil. Reduce the heat to low and simmer for 10 to 15 minutes. Season with salt and pepper to taste.

If you plan to simmer the chili for longer than 15 minutes, cover it tightly until you are ready to serve it.

Serve Four-Bean Chili warm in serving bowls with a dollop of sour cream on each serving.

Makes 4 servings

Cost $4.00

FRUGAL FACT: *Make this chili for even less by cooking your own beans. About ¾ cup dried beans will yield 2 cups of cooked beans.*

SLOW COOKER ADAPTABLE

FREEZER FRIENDLY

Southwest Chicken Chili

1 tablespoon extra-virgin olive oil ($.05)

2 boneless, skinless chicken breasts, about 1 pound, cut into bite-size pieces ($1.88)

1 small yellow onion, chopped ($.20)

1 can (15 ounces) corn kernels, drained ($.50)

1 can (15 ounces) pinto beans, rinsed and drained ($.68)

1 cup store-bought salsa or Homemade Salsa Fresca (page 260) ($.75)

1 cup store-bought or Homemade Chicken Stock (page 256) (free, if homemade)

2½ cups hot water

½ teaspoon ground cumin ($.03)

½ teaspoon chipotle chili powder ($.02)

½ teaspoon garlic powder ($.03)

Salt and pepper

½ cup brown rice ($.20)

½ cup shredded Monterey Jack cheese ($.32)

Sour cream for serving ($.10)

In a large pot or Dutch oven over medium-high heat, warm the olive oil. Add the chicken pieces and sauté until cooked through.

Add the onion, corn, pinto beans, salsa, and chicken stock. Stir in the water, along with the cumin, chipotle chili powder, garlic powder, and salt and pepper to taste. Stir in the rice and bring to a boil. Reduce the heat to medium, cover, and let cook for 45 to 50 minutes until the rice is tender.

Spoon the chili into serving bowls and add a pinch of cheese and a dollop of sour cream to each bowl.

Serve Southwest Chicken Chili.

Makes 4 servings

Cost $4.76 (Note: The cost will change with the substitution of store-bought salsa and/or chicken stock.)

FRUGAL FACT: *Shave off a few minutes of prep time on this recipe by using 1 cup frozen chopped onions, and shave off a few pennies by using your own batch-cooked pinto beans (page 16).*

SLOW COOKER ADAPTABLE

FREEZER FRIENDLY

Spinach and Bacon Chili

¾ pound ground beef ($1.12)

4 strips bacon, cooked and crumbled ($.50)

1 can (15 ounces) crushed tomatoes ($.20)

2 cups cooked red beans ($.40)

1 tablespoon chili powder ($.15)

1 teaspoon garlic powder ($.05)

1 teaspoon onion powder ($.05)

1 cup hot water

8 ounces fresh spinach leaves ($1)

Salt and pepper

French bread ($.50)

In a large pot or Dutch oven over medium-high heat, brown the ground beef. Drain and return it to the pot.

Add the bacon, crushed tomatoes, red beans, chili powder, garlic powder, and onion powder. Bring to a boil. Add the hot water and the spinach leaves, and stir as the spinach leaves "melt" into the chili.

Bring the chili back to a boil. Reduce the heat to medium-low, season with salt and pepper to taste, and let simmer for 20 minutes. If you plan to simmer it longer than 20 minutes, cover the chili tightly with a lid.

Serve the Spinach and Bacon Chili warm with sliced French bread.

Makes 4 servings

Cost $3.97 (Note: The cost will change with the substitution of canned beans.)

FRUGAL FACT: *Use up the spinach that you found for a reduced price in this simple chili—it's sure to become a family favorite!*

SLOW COOKER ADAPTABLE

FREEZER FRIENDLY

Green Pepper Chili

1 pound ground beef ($1.49)

½ small red onion, diced ($.20)

2 garlic cloves, crushed ($.05)

2 green bell peppers, seeded and diced ($1.18)

1 can (15 ounces) diced tomatoes, with their juices ($.20)

1 can (6 ounces) tomato paste ($.19)

2 cups cooked black beans ($.40)

2 cups cooked red beans ($.40)

1 tablespoon chili powder ($.15)

Salt and pepper

Fresh fruit, such as cantaloupe or orange wedges ($.50)

In a large pot or Dutch oven over medium-high heat, brown the ground beef with the onion and garlic. Drain and return the mixture to the pot.

Stir in the bell peppers, diced tomatoes, tomato paste, plus two 6-ounce cans' worth of water, the black beans, red beans, chili powder, and salt and pepper to taste. Bring to a boil. Reduce the heat to medium-low and simmer for 10 minutes. If you need to simmer the chili longer, cover it tightly to prevent too much liquid from cooking off. Remove from the heat and serve warm.

Serve Green Pepper Chili with fresh fruit.

Makes 4 servings

Cost $4.81 (Note: The cost will change with the substitution of canned beans.)

FRUGAL FACT: *Save time and substitute one 15-ounce can black beans and one 15-ounce can red kidney beans, both rinsed and drained.*

SLOW COOKER ADAPTABLE

FREEZER FRIENDLY

Barbecue Bean Chili

¾ pound ground beef ($1.12)

1 small yellow onion, chopped ($.20)

1 can (28 ounces) baked beans ($1.67)

4 carrots, peeled and diced ($.40)

1 can (15 ounces) diced tomatoes, with their juices ($.20)

1 can (8 ounces) tomato sauce ($.33)

1 cup water

2 tablespoons brown sugar ($.02)

2 tablespoons chili powder ($.20)

½ teaspoon crushed red pepper flakes ($.03)

French bread and butter ($.50)

In a large pot or Dutch oven over medium-high heat, sauté the ground beef with the onion. Drain and return the mixture to the pot.

Stir in the baked beans, carrots, diced tomatoes, tomato sauce, and water. Stir in the brown sugar, chili powder, and red pepper flakes. Reduce the heat to medium-low and simmer for 25 to 30 minutes.

Serve Barbecue Bean Chili warm with sliced French bread.

Makes 4 servings

Cost $4.67

FRUGAL FACT: *The best prices on baked beans can be found around the Memorial Day and Independence Day holidays. Stock up during the summer and you won't have to pay full price in the fall when you want to make this warm, hearty but "summery" chili.*

SLOW COOKER ADAPTABLE

FREEZER FRIENDLY

Black Bean Chili

1 pound dried black beans ($.99)

1 can (10 ounces) diced tomatoes with green chilies, with their juices ($.50)

1 small yellow onion, chopped ($.20)

1 cup frozen chopped green bell pepper ($.40)

2 cups store-bought or Homemade Chicken Stock (page 256) (free, if homemade) or Vegetable Stock (page 258) (free, if homemade)

1 to 2 cups water

1 teaspoon garlic powder ($.05)

1 teaspoon ground cumin ($.05)

Salt and pepper

½ cup brown rice ($.20)

Sour cream for serving ($.10)

Rinse the dried beans with cold water. Place in a large bowl, cover with cold water, and let soak overnight.

The next day, rinse the soaked beans and add them to a 5-quart or larger slow cooker with enough water to cover them by 1 inch. Set the slow cooker on high and cook for 4 hours.

Once the cooking cycle is complete, add the diced tomatoes with green chilies, onion, bell pepper, chicken stock or vegetable stock, and water. Stir in the garlic powder, cumin, and salt and pepper to taste. Reset the slow cooker to low and cook for 4 hours.

When there are 2 hours remaining in the cooking cycle, add the rice and continue to cook until the rice is tender. Remove the chili from the slow cooker to prevent the rice from overcooking with the residual heat of the slow cooker.

Serve Black Bean Chili warm with a dollop of sour cream in each serving bowl.

Makes 4 servings

Cost $2.69 (Note: The cost will change with the substitution of canned beans and/or store-bought chicken stock.)

FRUGAL FACT: *This black bean chili can also be made on the stovetop with about 6 cups of cooked black beans, or four 15-ounce cans of black beans. Simply add all the ingredients listed plus 2 cups of water to a Dutch oven, bring to a boil and simmer for 1 hour, or until the rice is tender.*

SLOW COOKER ADAPTABLE

FREEZER FRIENDLY

Tuscan Minestrone Soup

1 tablespoon extra-virgin olive oil ($.05)

1 small yellow onion, chopped ($.20)

2 garlic cloves, crushed ($.05)

1 large zucchini, about 1 pound, diced ($.79)

3 medium carrots, peeled and diced ($.30)

4 cups store-bought or Homemade Chicken Stock (page 256) (free, if homemade)

1 can (8 ounces) tomato sauce ($.33)

1 can (15 ounces) cannellini beans, rinsed and drained ($.67)

1 cup elbow macaroni ($.13)

1 cup hot water

1 teaspoon dried Italian seasoning ($.05)

½ cup grated Parmesan cheese ($.50)

Salt and pepper

Bread and butter ($.50)

In a large pot or Dutch oven over medium-high heat, warm the olive oil. Add the onion and garlic and sauté for 2 to 3 minutes. Add the zucchini and carrots and sauté for another 2 to 3 minutes. Add the chicken stock and tomato sauce and stir well.

Bring to a boil and add the cannellini beans, the macaroni, and the hot water. Stir in the Italian seasoning and salt and pepper to taste. Bring back to a boil and cook for 10 to 12 minutes until the pasta is al dente. Remove from the heat and serve warm.

Serve Tuscan Minestrone Soup with a side of bread and butter.

Makes 4 servings

Cost $3.57 (Note: The cost will change with the substitution of store-bought chicken stock.)

SLOW COOKER ADAPTABLE

FREEZER FRIENDLY

South-of-the-Border Chicken Soup

....

1 tablespoon extra-virgin olive
   oil ($.05)

1 small yellow onion, chopped ($.20)

2 chicken breasts, about 1 pound, cut
   into bite-size pieces ($1.88)

1 teaspoon garlic powder ($.05)

2 cups store-bought or Homemade
   Chicken Stock (page 256) (free, if
   homemade)

2 cups hot water

¼ cup lime juice ($.10)

1 can (15 ounces) corn kernels ($.50)

1 can (15 ounces) black beans ($.68)

½ cup brown rice ($.20)

Salt and pepper

1 avocado, seeded and sliced ($.75)

Sour cream for serving ($.10)

In a large pot or Dutch oven over medium-high heat, warm the olive oil. Add the onion, chicken pieces, and garlic powder and sauté for 7 to 9 minutes until the chicken has cooked through.

Stir in the chicken stock, hot water, and lime juice. Add the corn, beans, and rice, season with salt and pepper to taste, and bring to a boil. Reduce the heat to low, cover, and simmer for 45 to 50 minutes until the rice is tender. Remove from the heat and serve warm.

Serve South-of-the-Border Chicken Soup with a few avocado slices and a dollop of sour cream in each serving bowl.

Makes 4 servings

Cost $4.51 (Note: The cost will change with the substitution of store-bought chicken stock.)

FRUGAL FACT: *If you don't use all the avocado, rinse the remaining avocado under cold water, then store with the seed still nestled inside. This will keep it from browning, so you can use the rest the next day.*

SLOW COOKER ADAPTABLE

FREEZER FRIENDLY

Sausage Black Bean Soup

1 tablespoon extra-virgin olive oil ($.05)

1 red bell pepper, seeded and cut into bite-size pieces ($1)

3 bulk sausage links, about ¾ pound, sliced into ½-inch rounds ($1.67)

3 cups cooked black beans ($.60)

1 can (10 ounces) diced tomatoes with green chilies, with their juices ($.50)

4 cups hot water

½ cup brown rice ($.20)

1 teaspoon ground cumin ($.05)

Salt and pepper

Bread and butter ($.50)

In a large pot or Dutch oven over medium-high heat, warm the olive oil. Add the bell pepper and sausage rounds and sauté for 3 to 5 minutes.

Add the beans, diced tomatoes with green chilies, and the hot water. Stir in the rice. Add the cumin and a few dashes of salt and pepper, and bring to a boil. Reduce the heat to medium, cover, and cook for 45 to 50 minutes until the rice is tender. Remove from the heat and serve warm.

Serve Sausage Black Bean Soup with bread and butter.

Makes 4 servings

Cost $4.57 (Note: The cost will change with the substitution of canned beans.)

FRUGAL FACT: *Save some time and substitute two 15-ounce cans of black beans, undrained, for the 3 cups of cooked black beans in the recipe.*

SLOW COOKER ADAPTABLE

FREEZER FRIENDLY

Savory Chicken and White Bean Soup

1 tablespoon extra-virgin olive oil ($.05)

4 carrots, peeled and chopped ($.40)

3 celery stalks, chopped ($.30)

2 chicken breasts, about 1 pound, cut into bite-size pieces ($1.88)

1 can (15 ounces) white beans, rinsed and drained ($.68)

1 can (15 ounces) tomato sauce ($.20)

1 cup store-bought or Homemade Chicken Stock (page 256) (free, if homemade)

2 cups hot water

1 teaspoon dried parsley ($.05)

½ teaspoon dried thyme ($.03)

Salt and pepper

Bread and butter ($.50)

In a large pot or Dutch oven over medium-high heat, warm the olive oil. Add the carrots, celery, and chicken pieces and sauté for 7 to 9 minutes until the chicken has cooked through.

Stir in the white beans, tomato sauce, chicken stock, hot water, parsley, and thyme. Season with salt and pepper to taste and bring to a boil. Reduce the heat to low and simmer for 15 to 20 minutes. Remove from the heat and serve warm.

Serve Savory Chicken and White Bean Soup with bread and butter.

Makes 4 servings

Cost $4.09 (Note: The price will change with the substitution of store-bought chicken stock.)

FRUGAL FACT: *Get dinner on the table in less than 30 minutes with this simple, delicious soup.*

SLOW COOKER ADAPTABLE

FREEZER FRIENDLY

Hearty Sausage and Cabbage Stew

1 pound ground Italian sausage
meat ($2)

8 cups water

4 carrots, peeled and chopped ($.40)

4 celery stalks, peeled and
chopped ($.40)

1 small yellow onion, chopped ($.20)

4 cups chopped cabbage ($.50)

½ cup white rice ($.10)

1 teaspoon thyme ($.10)

Salt and pepper

In a large pot or Dutch oven over medium-high heat, brown the sausage meat.

When the meat has browned and is no longer pink, add the water plus the carrots, celery, onion, and cabbage and bring to a boil. Add the rice, thyme, and salt and pepper to taste. Reduce the heat to low, cover and simmer for 20 minutes, or until the rice is tender. Remove from the heat and serve warm.

Serve Hearty Sausage and Cabbage Stew.

Makes 4 servings

Cost $3.70

FRUGAL FACT: *Make it a habit to buy and use cabbage when you see it on sale for $.49 per pound or less.*

Beef and Barley Stew with Mushrooms

....

1 tablespoon extra-virgin olive
   oil ($.05)
¾ pound stew beef ($2.24)
½ small red onion, chopped ($.20)
2 garlic cloves, crushed ($.05)
2 cups store-bought or Homemade
   Beef Broth (page 257) (free, if
   homemade)

2 to 2½ cups hot water
½ cup pearled barley ($.25)
1 can (15 ounces) mushrooms,
   drained ($.99)
1 teaspoon dried parsley ($.05)
Salt and pepper

Bread and butter ($.50)

In a large pot or Dutch oven over high heat, warm the olive oil. Add the beef
cubes and brown on all sides. Once browned, add the onion and garlic and sauté
with the beef for 4 to 5 minutes. Stir in the beef broth and hot water and bring
to a boil.

Add the pearled barley, mushrooms, and the parsley and return to a boil. Reduce the heat to medium or medium-low and cook at a rolling boil for 40 to 45
minutes until the barley is tender. Season with salt and pepper to taste. Remove
from the heat and serve warm.

Serve Beef and Barley Stew with Mushrooms with bread and butter.

Makes 4 servings

Cost $4.33 (Note: The cost will change with the substitution of store-bought
beef broth.)

FRUGAL FACT: *You can substitute 1 pound of fresh sliced mushrooms for the
canned mushrooms when you see them at a reduced-for-quick-sale price.*

Beef, Chickpea, and Spinach Stew

1 tablespoon extra-virgin olive
   oil ($.05)
¾ pound stew beef ($2.24)
1 small white onion, chopped ($.20)
2 garlic cloves, crushed ($.05)
1 can (15 ounces) tomato sauce ($.20)
5 cups hot water

2 cans (15 ounces) chickpeas, rinsed
   and drained ($1.36)
1 box (10 ounces) frozen chopped
   spinach ($.50)
1 teaspoon ground ginger ($.05)
1 teaspoon ground cumin ($.05)
Salt and pepper

In a large pot or Dutch oven over medium-high heat, warm the olive oil. Add the stew beef and brown on all sides. Add the onion and garlic, and cook for 5 minutes.

Add the tomato sauce and the hot water and bring to a boil. Stir in the chickpeas, spinach, ginger, and cumin and return to a boil.

Reduce the heat to low, cover, and simmer for 15 to 20 minutes. Season with salt and pepper to taste. Remove from the heat and serve warm.

Serve Beef, Chickpea, and Spinach Stew.

Makes 4 servings

Cost $4.70

FRUGAL FACT: *Cook your own dried chickpeas, using the same procedure as cooking dried beans (see page 16).*

SLOW COOKER ADAPTABLE

FREEZER FRIENDLY

Mango Lentil Stew

7 cups water

2 cups green lentils ($1)

2 garlic cloves, crushed ($.05)

4 small Idaho potatoes, peeled and diced ($.60)

4 carrots, peeled and diced ($.40)

1 small yellow onion, chopped ($.20)

2 tablespoons brown sugar ($.02)

1 tablespoon curry powder ($.15)

2 mangoes, seeded, peeled and diced ($1.98)

In a large pot or Dutch oven over high heat, bring the water to a boil. Add the lentils, garlic, potatoes, carrots, onion, brown sugar, and curry powder and return to a boil. Reduce the heat to low, cover, and simmer for 15 to 20 minutes until the lentils and potatoes are tender.

Add the mango to the stew and simmer for 8 to 10 minutes longer. Remove from the heat and serve warm.

Serve Mango Lentil Stew.

Makes 4 servings

Cost $4.40

FRUGAL FACT: *This flavorful vegetarian stew, made for less than $5, will not disappoint.*

Slow Cooker Beef and Vegetable Stew

1 pound cooked ground beef ($1.49)

1 can (4 ounces) sliced mushrooms, undrained ($.49)

1 can (15 ounces) stewed tomatoes, with their juices ($.20)

1 can (8 ounces) tomato sauce ($.33)

1 bag (12 ounces) frozen vegetable soup mix ($.88)

1 teaspoon dried Italian seasoning ($.05)

4 cups hot water

1½ cups small shell pasta ($.25)

Salt and pepper

¼ cup grated Parmesan cheese, for serving ($.25)

Place all of the ingredients, except for the pasta, salt and pepper, and cheese in the insert of a 5-quart or larger slow cooker, set on high and cook for 4 hours, or set on low and cook for 8 hours.

When there is 30 minutes remaining in the cooking cycle, add the pasta. If using "quick-cooking" pasta and the package indicates it only needs 7 minutes to cook, then add it when there is 20 minutes left in the cooking cycle. Season with salt and pepper to taste.

When the stew has finished cooking and the pasta is al dente, serve the stew immediately, or transfer to a large serving bowl so the pasta will not overcook from the residual heat of the slow cooker.

Serve Slow Cooker Beef and Vegetable Stew sprinkled with Parmesan cheese.

Makes 4 servings

Cost $3.94

FRUGAL FACT: *Watch the national drugstores for the best prices on cans of sliced mushrooms and tomato sauce.*

Slow Cooker Black Bean and Sausage Stew

4 cups cooked black beans ($.80)

1 pound mild Italian sausage links, sliced into 1-inch rounds ($2.99)

1 box (10 ounces) frozen chopped spinach ($.50)

1 can (10 ounces) diced tomatoes with green chilies, with their juices ($.20)

2 cups store-bought or Homemade Chicken Stock (page 256) (free, if homemade)

4 cups hot water

Salt and pepper

Sour cream for serving ($.10)

Put the cooked beans, sausage, spinach, and diced tomatoes with green chilies into the insert of a 5-quart or larger slow cooker. (If you prefer, you can substitute two 15-ounce cans of black beans for the 3 cups cooked black beans.) Add the stock and hot water and stir to combine all of the ingredients.

Set the slow cooker on low and cook for 8 hours. Season with salt and pepper to taste. Let cool slightly before serving.

Serve Slow Cooker Black Bean and Sausage Stew with a dollop of sour cream in each serving bowl.

Makes 4 servings

Cost $4.59 (Note: The cost will change with the substitution of canned beans and/or store-bought chicken stock.)

FRUGAL FACT: *By letting the slow cooker do all the work for you, you can get dinner on the table with less than 5 minutes of prep time.*

FREEZER FRIENDLY

Chorizo Black Bean Soup

1 pound chorizo Mexican
    sausage ($2.99)

4 cups cooked black beans ($.60)

1 cup store-bought or Homemade
    Chicken Stock (page 256) (free, if
    homemade)

4 cups hot water

½ cup frozen chopped green bell
    pepper ($.20)

1 can (10 ounces) diced tomatoes
    with green chilies, with their juices
    ($.50)

1 can (15 ounces) corn kernels, with
    their liquid ($.50)

1 tablespoon minced onion ($.10)

1 teaspoon ground cumin ($.05)

Salt and pepper

In a large pot or Dutch oven over medium-high heat, brown the chorizo. Drain and return it to the pot.

Add the beans, chicken stock, and water. Stir in the bell pepper, diced tomatoes with green chilies, and corn. Stir in the onion, cumin, and salt and pepper to taste and bring to a boil. Reduce the heat to low, and simmer for 15 to 20 minutes. Remove from the heat and serve warm.

Serve Chorizo Black Bean Soup.

Makes 4 servings

Cost $4.94 (Note: The cost will change with the substitution of canned beans and/or store-bought chicken stock.)

FRUGAL FACT: *To make this in the slow cooker, brown the sausage in a skillet or sauté pan before adding it to the slow cooker. Stir in all of the ingredients in the slow cooker, set on low, and cook for 8 to 10 hours.*

SLOW COOKER ADAPTABLE

FREEZER FRIENDLY

Vegetable Fiesta Stew

1 tablespoon extra-virgin olive oil ($.05)

1 small red onion, chopped ($.40)

2 garlic cloves, crushed ($.05)

3 cups green cabbage, shredded ($.50)

3 cups cooked black beans ($.60)

1 can (10 ounces) diced tomatoes with green chilies, with their juices ($.50)

2 potatoes, peeled and diced ($.30)

1 cup store-bought or Homemade Chicken Stock (page 256) (free, if homemade)

4 cups hot water

Salt and pepper

Bread and butter ($.50)

In a large pot or Dutch oven over medium-high heat, warm the olive oil. Add the onion and garlic and sauté for 2 or 3 minutes. Add the cabbage and sauté with the onion and garlic for 2 minutes more.

Add the beans, diced tomatoes with green chilies, potatoes, chicken stock, and hot water and bring to a boil. Reduce the heat to medium, cover, and cook for 20 to 30 minutes until the potatoes are soft and the flavors have mingled. Season with salt and pepper to taste.

Serve Vegetable Fiesta Stew with bread and butter.

Makes 4 servings.

Cost $2.90 (Note: The cost will change with the substitution of canned beans and/or store-bought chicken stock.)

FRUGAL FACT: *When you see cabbage on sale at the store, plan to add 2 or 3 meals to your weekly meal plan that week that will allow you to use the entire head of cabbage. A single cabbage head can yield up to 8 cups shredded cabbage, so make a stew like this one, as well as some coleslaw and another soup like Hearty Sausage and Cabbage Stew (page 202).*

Chunky Split Pea Soup

5 Italian sausage links, about 1 pound, sliced ($2.99)

6 medium white Idaho potatoes, peeled and diced ($.80)

4 carrot sticks, peeled and chopped ($.40)

1 small yellow onion, chopped ($.20)

1 teaspoon garlic powder ($.05)

1 teaspoon parsley ($.05)

2 cups store-bought or Homemade Chicken Stock (page 256) (free, if homemade)

2 to 3 cups hot water

1½ cups green split peas, about ½ pound ($.50)

Salt and pepper

In a large pot or Dutch oven over medium-high heat, brown the sausage pieces for 4 to 5 minutes. Drain and return them to the pot.

Add the potatoes, carrots, and onion to the sausage and sauté for 5 to 7 minutes, stirring often, until the onions are translucent.

Stir in the garlic powder, parsley, broth, hot water, and the split peas and bring to a boil. Reduce the heat to low and simmer for 50 minutes. Season with salt and pepper to taste.

Serve Chunky Split Pea Soup.

Makes 4 servings

Cost $4.99 (Note: The cost will change with the substitution of store-bought chicken stock.)

FRUGAL FACT: *My "never-pay-more-than" price for an 18-ounce package of Italian sausage or bratwurst sausage is $2.99.*

Santa Fe Minestrone

1 pound ground beef ($1.49)

2 garlic cloves, crushed ($.05)

1 small yellow onion, chopped ($.20)

4 carrots, peeled and chopped ($.40)

2 celery stalks, chopped ($.20)

1 can (10 ounces) diced tomatoes with green chilies, with their juices ($.50)

1 can (15 ounces) black beans, rinsed and drained ($.68)

2 cups store-bought or Homemade Beef Broth (page 257) (free, if homemade)

4 cups hot water

2 teaspoons Homemade Taco Seasoning (page 266) ($.07)

Salt and pepper

2 cups small shell pasta ($.25)

Sour cream for serving ($.10)

In a large pot or Dutch oven over medium-high heat, brown the ground beef with the garlic and onions. Drain and return the mixture to the pot.

Add the carrots, celery, diced tomatoes with green chilies, beans, beef broth, and hot water. Stir in the taco seasoning, and salt and pepper to taste and bring to a boil. Reduce the heat to medium and add the pasta. Cook for 9 to 11 minutes until the pasta is al dente. Let cool slightly before serving.

Serve Santa Fe Minestrone with a dollop of sour cream in each serving bowl.

Makes 4 servings

Cost $3.94 (Note: The cost will change with the substitution of store-bought beef broth.)

FRUGAL FACT: *A Tex-Mex spin on the traditional Italian minestrone soup, this recipe uses mostly pantry staple ingredients.*

SLOW COOKER ADAPTABLE

FREEZER FRIENDLY

Spinach and Lentil Soup

1 tablespoon extra-virgin olive oil ($.05)

1 small yellow onion, chopped ($.20)

2 garlic cloves, crushed ($.05)

1 can (10 ounces) diced tomatoes with green chilies ($.50)

1 can (8 ounces) tomato sauce ($.33)

2 cups store-bought or Homemade Chicken Stock (page 256) (free, if homemade) or Vegetable Stock (page 258) (free, if homemade)

6 cups hot water

1 box (10 ounces) frozen chopped spinach ($.50)

1 cup white rice ($.20)

1½ cups green lentils ($.75)

Salt and pepper

In a large pot or Dutch oven over medium-high heat, warm the olive oil. Add the onion and garlic and sauté for 2 to 3 minutes. Stir in the diced tomatoes with green chilies, tomato sauce, chicken or vegetable stock, and hot water. Stir in the frozen spinach and stir, breaking it up in the stew as it defrosts. Bring to a boil.

Add the rice and green lentils and return to a rolling boil. Reduce the heat to medium-low and cook for 15 to 20 minutes until the lentils and rice are both tender. Season with salt and pepper to taste.

Serve Spinach and Lentil Soup.

Makes 4 servings

Cost $2.78 (Note: The cost will change with the substitution of store-bought chicken or vegetable stock.)

FRUGAL FACT: *Even if you use store-bought chicken broth, you can still make this meal for well under $5.*

Sausage and Spinach Minestra

3 bulk sausage links, about ¾ pound, sliced into ¼-inch rounds ($1.67)

4 cups store-bought or Homemade Chicken Stock (page 256) (free, if homemade) or Vegetable Stock (page 258) (free, if homemade)

2½ cups hot water

1 can (15 ounces) diced tomatoes, with their juices ($.20)

1 box (10 ounces) frozen chopped spinach ($.50)

½ cup chopped onion ($.20)

1 teaspoon dried Italian seasoning ($.05)

½ teaspoon garlic salt ($.02)

Black pepper

1½ cup small shells pasta ($.20)

Bread slices and butter ($.50)

To a 5-quart or larger slow cooker, add the broth plus 2 cups of the hot water. Stir in the diced tomatoes, frozen spinach, and onion. Add the sausage slices, Italian seasoning, garlic salt, and pepper to taste.

Set the slow cooker on low and cook for 8 hours. Thirty minutes before serving time, mix in the pasta and the remaining ½ cup hot water. When the pasta is al dente, serve the soup immediately or transfer to a tureen or large serving bowl to prevent the pasta from overcooking from the residual heat of the slow cooker.

Serve Sausage and Spinach Minestra with bread and butter.

Makes 4 servings

Cost $3.74 (Note: The cost will change with the substitution of store-bought chicken or vegetable stock.)

FRUGAL FACT: *If you are at home and/or forgot to start the slow cooker, you can cook this soup on high for 4 hours instead of on low for 8 hours.*

SLOW COOKER ADAPTABLE

FREEZER FRIENDLY

Vegetable Minestrone Soup

2 bags (12 ounces each) frozen
  vegetable soup mix ($1.60)
1 can (15 ounces) diced tomatoes,
  with their juices ($.20)
1 can (15 ounces) crushed
  tomatoes ($.20)
5 cups hot water

2 cups cooked red kidney beans ($.40)
4 garlic cloves, crushed ($.10)
½ teaspoon dried Italian
  seasoning ($.03)
Salt and pepper
2 cups small shell pasta ($.25)

Bread slices and butter ($.50)

To a 5-quart or larger slow cooker, add the frozen vegetable soup mix, the diced tomatoes, and the crushed tomatoes plus 4 cups of the hot water. Stir in the kidney beans, garlic, and Italian seasoning. Season with salt and pepper to taste. Set the slow cooker on high and cook for 4 hours.

About 30 minutes before serving the soup, add the pasta with the remaining 1 cup hot water to the slow cooker. When the pasta is al dente, serve the soup immediately, or transfer to a tureen or large serving bowl to prevent the pasta from overcooking from the residual heat of the slow cooker.

Serve Vegetable Minestrone Soup with bread and butter.

Makes 4 servings

Cost $3.28 (Note: The cost will change with the substitution of canned beans.)

FRUGAL FACT: *To cook this soup in a Dutch oven, place all the ingredients into the Dutch oven in the order listed, except for the pasta. Bring to a boil and cook for 20 minutes. Add the pasta with 1 cup hot water and cook for 8 to 10 minutes more, or until the pasta is al dente.*

FREEZER FRIENDLY

TEN

Vegetarian One-Dish Dinners

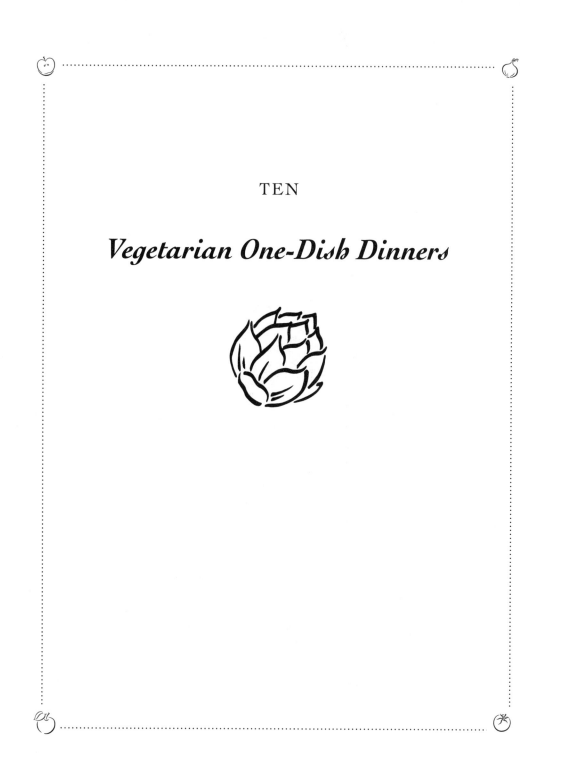

Zucchini, Red Pepper, and Avocado Frittata

1 tablespoon extra-virgin olive
    oil ($.05)

½ small red onion, chopped ($.20)

2 small zucchini, about 1 pound,
    diced ($.79)

1 red bell pepper, seeded and
    diced ($1)

8 eggs ($.80)

½ cup milk ($.05)

¼ teaspoon ground cumin ($.01)

Salt and pepper

1 avocado, seeded and diced ($.75)

1 cup pepper jack blend shredded
    cheese ($.67)

Fresh fruit, such as apple slices or orange wedges ($.50)

Preheat the oven to 350 degrees.

In a large 12-inch skillet or sauté pan over medium-high heat, warm the olive oil. Add the onion, zucchini, and bell pepper and sauté for 4 to 5 minutes until the onion is translucent and the zucchini and pepper have softened.

Meanwhile, in a mixing bowl, whisk together the eggs and milk and add the cumin, salt, and pepper.

Reduce the heat to medium and pour the egg mixture over the sautéed vegetables in the skillet. Quickly float the diced avocado in the egg mixture. Cook the frittata on the stovetop for about 3 minutes, or until you see the eggs begin to set around the edges of the skillet.

Transfer the skillet to the preheated oven and bake for 15 to 20 minutes until the eggs in the middle have set.

Sprinkle the shredded cheese on the top and bake for 5 minutes more, or until the cheese has melted.

Once the cheese has melted, carefully remove the skillet from the oven. Be sure to use heavy-duty oven mitts as the handle will be hot. Let cool slightly before slicing and serving.

Serve Zucchini, Red Pepper, and Avocado Frittata with a side of fresh fruit.

Makes 4 servings

Cost $4.82

FRUGAL FACT: *Stock up on zucchini when you see a price of $.79 per pound or less. Use what you can that week, and then dice and grate the rest and freeze. Frozen grated zucchini is perfect for making zucchini bread and muffins and for soup or chili recipes like Zucchini Chicken Chili (page 186).*

Roasted Vegetable and Herb Medley

1 small red onion, diced ($.40)

2 celery stalks, sliced into ¼-inch slices ($.20)

2 small zucchini, about 1 pound, sliced into ½-inch rounds ($.79)

4 carrots, peeled and sliced into 1-inch rounds ($.40)

½ pound radishes (about 15), stems removed, quartered ($.50)

2 plum tomatoes, quartered ($1)

4 medium Idaho potatoes, cut into ½-inch chunks ($.60)

3 tablespoons extra-virgin olive oil ($.15)

1 teaspoon dried parsley leaves ($.05)

1 teaspoon dried basil leaves ($.05)

½ teaspoon dried oregano leaves ($.03)

Salt and pepper

Bread and butter ($.50)

Preheat the oven to 400 degrees. Grease a 9 × 13-inch glass baking dish with nonstick cooking spray.

Put the onion, celery, zucchini, carrots, radishes, tomatoes, and potatoes in the prepared baking dish. Drizzle the olive oil over the vegetables and toss gently. Sprinkle the parsley, basil, oregano, and salt and pepper to taste over the vegetables and toss gently again.

Roast the vegetables in the preheated oven for 55 to 60 minutes until the larger potato pieces are soft when pierced with a knife.

Serve Roasted Vegetable and Herb Medley with bread and butter.

Makes 4 servings

Cost $4.67

FRUGAL FACT: *If you wish to use fresh parsley, basil, and oregano from the garden, chop the leaves and add them to the roasting vegetables for the last 10 minutes of cooking.*

MAKE-AHEAD MEAL

Bean Enchilada Casserole

3 cups cooked red beans ($.60)

3 cups cooked black beans ($.60)

1 can (15 ounce) corn kernels, drained ($.50)

1 can (10 ounces) diced tomatoes with green chilies, drained ($.50)

1 can (8 ounces) tomato sauce ($.33)

1 tablespoon Homemade Taco Seasoning (page 266) ($.10)

10 corn tortillas ($.69)

2 cups shredded Mexican blend cheese ($1.25)

Preheat the oven to 350 degrees. Grease a 9 × 13-inch glass baking dish with nonstick cooking spray.

In a mixing bowl, combine the red beans, black beans, corn, and diced tomatoes with green chilies, tomato sauce, and taco seasoning.

Spoon about half of the bean mixture into the bottom of the prepared baking dish. Top with 5 of the corn tortillas, ripping one in half, if necessary, to cover the middle. Sprinkle half of the shredded cheese over the tortillas. Repeat the layering with the remaining bean mixture, the remaining 5 tortillas, and the remaining cheese.

Bake in the preheated oven for 15 to 20 minutes until the mixture is bubbling and the cheese has melted. Let cool slightly before cutting and serving.

Serve Bean Enchilada Casserole.

Makes 4 servings

Cost $4.57 (Note: The cost will change with the substitution of canned beans.)

FRUGAL FACT: *Using dried beans that you have cooked, or better yet batch cooked, is the only way to keep this casserole under $5. You could save time and use two 15-ounce cans each of the black and red beans, but the cost of the beans will almost double the cost of the meal, making it much more than $5.*

FREEZER FRIENDLY

Black Bean and Rice Bake with "Piña de Gallo"

3 cups cooked black beans ($.60)

1¼ cups brown rice ($.50)

1 cup store-bought or Homemade Chicken Stock (page 256) (free, if homemade) or Vegetable Stock (page 258) (free, if homemade))

2 cups hot water

2 garlic cloves, crushed ($.05)

Salt and pepper

PIÑA DE GALLO

2 cups fresh pineapple, cut into bite-size pieces ($1)

1 plum tomato, seeded and diced ($.50)

1 small red onion, finely chopped ($.40)

3 sprigs fresh cilantro, chopped ($.25)

½ teaspoon ground cumin ($.03)

Salt and pepper

Preheat the oven to 350 degrees. Grease a 9 × 13-inch glass baking dish with nonstick cooking spray.

To the prepared baking dish, add the beans, rice, chicken or vegetable stock, and hot water. (If you prefer, you can substitute two 15-ounce cans of rinsed and drained black beans for the 3 cups cooked black beans.) Add the garlic and season with salt and pepper. Cover the baking dish tightly with aluminum foil.

Bake in the preheated oven for 60 minutes, or until the rice is tender.

Meanwhile, in a mixing bowl, toss together the pineapple, tomato, onion, cilantro, cumin, and salt and pepper to taste.

Serve Black Beans and Rice Bake with "Piña de Gallo" over the top.

Makes 4 servings

Cost $3.42 (Note: The cost will change with the substitution of canned beans and/or store-bought chicken or vegetable stock.)

FRUGAL FACT: *Use tomatoes and cilantro from the garden to cut the overall cost of this meal to less than $3 for 4 people.*

Red Beans and Rice with Pineapple

....

2 cans (15 ounces) dark red kidney
  beans, rinsed and drained ($1.36)
2 cans (20 ounces) pineapple chunks
  in pineapple juice ($1)
1½ cups brown rice ($.60)
2½ cups hot water

2 tablespoons chopped fresh cilantro
  leaves ($.20)
Garlic salt
Black pepper
½ teaspoon ground cumin ($.03)

Preheat the oven to 350 degrees. Grease a 9 × 13-inch glass baking dish with
nonstick cooking spray.

Add the beans to the prepared baking dish. (If you prefer to cook your own beans,
substitute 3 cups cooked red kidney beans.)

Drain ½ cup of the pineapple juice from the pineapple cans into a liquid measuring cup and reserve. Drain off the rest of the liquid and toss the pineapple
chunks with the beans in the baking dish. Sprinkle the rice over the top of the
beans and pineapple.

Pour the reserved pineapple juice and the hot water over the rice, beans, and
pineapple in the baking dish. Sprinkle the cilantro over the top. Sprinkle with
garlic salt and pepper. Cover the dish tightly with aluminum foil.

Bake in the preheated oven for 1 hour to 1 hour and 15 minutes until the rice is
tender. Remove the casserole from the oven and lightly toss the beans, rice,
and pineapple with a fork. Sprinkle with a little cumin. Let cool slightly before
serving.

Serve Red Beans and Rice with Pineapple.

Makes 4 servings

Cost $3.19

FRUGAL FACT: *Stock up on cans of pineapple chunks when their price hits $1 or less, and be sure to match with a coupon to get cans of pineapple for as little as $.50 each.*

Lentil Curry with Chickpeas, Carrots, and Spinach

....

1 tablespoon extra-virgin olive oil ($.05)

1 small red onion, chopped ($.40)

4 garlic cloves, crushed ($.10)

4½ cups hot water

1½ cups green lentils ($.75)

1 cup white rice ($.20)

3 carrots, peeled and diced ($.30)

1 can (15 ounces) crushed tomatoes ($.20)

1 can (15 ounces) chickpeas, rinsed and drained ($.68)

3 tablespoons curry powder ($.45)

8 ounces fresh spinach leaves ($1)

Salt and pepper

Crushed red pepper (optional) ($.05)

In a large pot or Dutch oven over medium-high heat, warm the olive oil. Add the onion and garlic and sauté for 2 to 3 minutes. Add the hot water and bring to a boil.

Add the lentils and the rice. Stir in the carrots, crushed tomatoes, and chickpeas and return to a boil.

Stir in the curry powder. Reduce the heat to medium, cover, and let cook for 20 minutes, or until the rice and lentils are tender.

Add the spinach leaves to the curry and let "melt" in with the rest of the ingredients, stirring once or twice. Season with salt and pepper to taste.

If you wish to add some additional heat to this curry, add some red pepper flakes.

Serve Lentil Curry with Chickpeas, Carrots, and Spinach.

Makes 4 servings

Cost $4.18

FRUGAL FACT: *Lentils and rice, when served together, form a complete protein. Combining legumes and grains together is an inexpensive and healthy way to get complete proteins into your daily diet.*

Southwest Barley Salad

....

1¼ cups pearled barley ($.75)

1 can (15 ounces) black beans, rinsed and drained ($.68)

1 can (15 ounces) corn kernels ($.50)

1 avocado, seeded and diced ($.75)

1½ tablespoons lime juice ($.03)

1 tablespoon olive oil ($.10)

1 tablespoon chopped fresh cilantro leaves ($.10)

Salt and pepper

In a large pot or Dutch oven over medium-high heat, cook the pearled barley as directed on the package. When cooked through and tender, drain and rinse with cold water.

Transfer the barley to a serving bowl and toss with the beans, corn, and avocado.

In a small mixing bowl, whisk together the lime juice, olive oil, cilantro, and salt and pepper to taste. Pour over the barley salad and toss well. Chill the salad in the refrigerator for at least 30 minutes.

Serve Southwest Barley Salad.

Makes 4 servings

Cost $2.91

FRUGAL FACT: *If you are in a time crunch, use quick-cooking barley to cut the barley cooking time by more than half.*

Fiesta Beans and Rice

3½ cups water

1½ cups brown rice ($.60)

2 cups cooked red beans ($.40)

1 red bell pepper, seeded and
   chopped ($1)

1 green bell pepper, seeded and
   chopped ($.59)

1 can (15 ounces) corn kernels ($.50)

1 can (8 ounces) tomato sauce ($.33)

1 teaspoon ground cumin ($.05)

Salt and pepper

In a large pot or Dutch oven over high heat, bring the water to a boil. Add the rice and return to a boil. Cover, reduce the heat to medium, and cook the rice for 45 to 50 minutes until tender.

Once the rice is cooked, stir in the beans, bell peppers, corn, tomato sauce, and cumin. Season with salt and pepper to taste.

If necessary, reduce the heat to low, cover, and keep warm until serving time.

Serve Fiesta Beans and Rice.

Makes 4 servings

Cost $3.47 (Note: The cost will change with the substitution of canned beans.)

FRUGAL FACT: *Just because you are on a rice-and-beans budget, doesn't mean you can't enjoy dinner. This is the perfect way to jazz up your next rice and beans meal.*

Chilled Tropical Rice and Bean Salad

....

4 cups water

2 tablespoons lime juice ($.10)

1 can (18 ounces) pineapple tidbits, drained, juice reserved ($.99)

2 cups white rice ($.40)

2 cans (15 ounces) small red beans, drained and rinsed ($1.36)

1 red bell pepper, seeded and diced ($1)

1 teaspoon ground cumin ($.05)

Salt and pepper

In a large pot or Dutch oven over high heat, bring the water, lime juice, and pineapple juice to a boil. (Reserve the pineapple tidbits.)

Add the rice and return to a boil. Reduce the heat, cover, and simmer for 15 to 20 minutes until the rice is tender. Remove the rice from the heat.

Toss the cooked rice with the red beans, the bell pepper, reserved pineapple tidbits, cumin, and some salt and pepper to taste.

Chill the salad in the refrigerator for at least 2 hours.

Serve Chilled Tropical Rice and Bean Salad.

Makes 4 servings

Cost $3.90

FRUGAL FACT: *Prepare this easy dinner while your kids are finishing their lunch, or enjoying their afternoon snack. If you don't have time to chill it in the refrigerator, then rinse the cooked rice with cool water in a colander before tossing in the remaining ingredients.*

Red Quinoa with Avocado, Black Beans, and Corn

....

1 tablespoon extra-virgin olive
   oil ($.05)

1 small red onion, chopped ($.40)

1 cup frozen diced green bell
   pepper ($.40)

1 cup frozen corn kernels ($.40)

2 tablespoons chopped fresh cilantro
   ($.20)

1 cup red quinoa ($1)

2 cups hot water

2 cups cooked black beans ($.40)

¼ cup lime juice ($.10)

Salt and pepper

1 avocado, diced ($.75)

In a large pot or Dutch oven over medium-high heat, warm the olive oil. Add the onion, bell pepper, corn, and cilantro and sauté for 5 to 7 minutes until the juices begin to thicken.

Add the quinoa and the hot water and bring to a boil. Cover, reduce the heat, and simmer for 15 minutes.

Once the ring has separated from the quinoa grains, add the beans and lime juice and simmer for 5 to 10 minutes more. Season with salt and pepper to taste. Garnish each serving bowl with the diced avocado.

Serve Red Quinoa with Avocado, Black Beans, and Corn.

Makes 4 servings

Cost $3.70 (Note: The price will change with the substitution of canned beans.)

FRUGAL FACT: *Look for the best prices on red quinoa on amazon.com, or at specialty or ethnic grocery stores.*

Spicy Quinoa with Corn, Beans, and Lime

2 cups store-bought vegetable broth or Homemade Vegetable Stock (page 258) ($1) (free, if homemade)

2 cups water

2 cups white quinoa ($1.60)

3 garlic cloves, crushed ($.08)

1 small red onion, finely chopped ($.40)

1 can (15 ounces) corn kernels, drained ($.50)

1 can (10 ounces) diced tomatoes with green chilies, with their juices ($.20)

1 can (15 ounces) red kidney beans, drained and rinsed ($.68)

1 teaspoon ground cumin ($.05)

Salt and pepper

Juice of 1 lime ($.33)

1 sprig fresh cilantro, chopped for garnish ($.12)

In a large pot or Dutch oven over high heat, bring the vegetable stock and water to a boil, stir in the quinoa, and return to a boil. Reduce the heat to medium, cover, and cook for 15 minutes.

Once the quinoa has cooked, add the garlic, onion, corn, diced tomatoes with green chilies, beans, cumin, and salt and pepper to taste.

Stir in the lime juice and simmer 5 to 7 minutes more. Remove from the heat and keep covered until ready to serve.

Serve Spicy Quinoa with Corn, Beans, and Lime with fresh chopped cilantro garnish.

Makes 4 servings

Cost $4.96 (Note: The cost will change with the substitution of store-bought vegetable stock and/or canned beans.)

FRUGAL FACT: *Use 4 cups of water, instead of 2 cups of vegetable stock and 2 cups of water to cut the overall cost of this meal by $1.*

Quinoa with Lentils and Apples

5 cups water

1 cup white quinoa ($.80)

1 cup green lentils ($.50)

1 small yellow onion, chopped ($.20)

4 carrots, peeled and chopped ($.40)

3 Golden Delicious apples, peeled and chopped ($.75)

1 teaspoon ground cumin ($.05)

1 teaspoon garlic powder ($.05)

Salt and pepper

Sour cream for serving ($.10)

In a large pot or Dutch oven over high heat, bring the water to a boil. Add the quinoa and lentils, reduce the heat to medium, cover, and cook for 15 to 20 minutes until the lentils have softened.

Remove the lid from the pot and add the onion, carrots, and apples. Stir in the cumin, garlic powder, and salt and pepper to taste. Turn off the heat and let the mixture sit for 10 minutes before serving.

Serve Quinoa with Lentils and Apples with a dollop of sour cream in each serving bowl.

Makes 4 servings

Cost $2.85

FRUGAL FACT: *Find the best price per pound for white quinoa in bulk at the warehouse clubs or on amazon.com.*

Four-Bean Quinoa Salad

2½ cups water

1 cup white quinoa ($.80)

1 can (15 ounces) green beans, drained and rinsed ($.50)

1 can (15 ounces) black beans, drained and rinsed ($.68)

1 can (15 ounces) red beans, drained and rinsed ($.68)

1 can (15 ounces) white beans, drained and rinsed ($.68)

DRESSING

¼ cup extra-virgin olive oil ($.20)

¼ cup red wine vinegar ($.20)

1 teaspoon dried Italian seasoning ($.05)

½ teaspoon salt

½ black pepper

In a large pot or Dutch oven over high heat, bring the water to a boil, add the quinoa, and return to a boil. Cover, reduce the heat, and cook for 15 minutes.

Once the quinoa has cooked, drain off any excess liquid. Then add the green beans, black beans, red beans, and white beans.

Stir in the olive oil, vinegar, Italian seasoning, and salt and pepper.

Chill the salad in the refrigerator for at least 2 hours. Toss well before serving.

Serve Four-Bean Quinoa Salad.

Makes 4 servings

Cost $3.79

FRUGAL FACT: *Make the most of your time in the kitchen by cooking the quinoa while your kids are eating breakfast or lunch, then toss together with the rest of the ingredients and place in the fridge. Then all you have to do is pull it out and set dinner on the table.*

Quinoa Chicken Primavera

2½ cups water

1 cup quinoa ($.75)

1 bag (12 ounces) frozen peas ($.80)

2 cups grilled chicken, diced ($1.50)

1 pint cherry or grape tomatoes, halved ($1.49)

2 ounces cream cheese, softened ($.25)

¼ cup milk ($.02)

1 teaspoon dried Italian seasoning ($.05)

2 garlic cloves, crushed ($.10)

Salt and pepper

In a large pot or Dutch oven, bring the water to a boil. Add the quinoa and return to a boil. Cover, reduce the heat, and cook for 15 minutes.

Cook the frozen peas as directed on the package.

Once the quinoa has cooked, drain any excess liquid. Add the chicken, peas, and cherry tomatoes.

In a small mixing bowl, whisk together the softened cream cheese, milk, Italian seasoning, and garlic. Pour the dressing over the quinoa mixture and season with salt and pepper to taste.

Chill the salad in the refrigerator for 2 hours.

Serve Quinoa Chicken Primavera.

Makes 4 servings

Cost $4.96

FRUGAL FACT: *Make this meal for less by using small tomatoes from your garden. Tomato plants grow easily in containers, for those who don't have space for a patio planter or in-ground garden.*

ELEVEN

One-Dish and One-Bowl Desserts

Mango-Raspberry Crumble

2 mangos, peeled, seeded and cut into
   1-inch chunks ($1.98)
1 pint raspberries ($1.50)

¼ cup brown sugar ($.06)
2 tablespoons all-purpose flour ($.02)

TOPPING

¾ cup all-purpose flour ($.15)
½ cup quick-cooking oats ($.12)
½ cup granulated sugar ($.05)

1 teaspoon salt
⅓ cup butter, cut into ½-inch
   pieces ($.53)

Ice cream or whipped topping ($.50)

Preheat the oven to 350 degrees. Grease a 9-inch glass pie plate with nonstick cooking spray.

Gently toss the mango chunks, raspberries, brown sugar, and flour in the prepared pie plate.

In a small mixing bowl, combine the flour, oats, granulated sugar, and salt. Cut the butter pieces into the dry ingredients with a pastry blender or fork until the mixture is crumbly. Pour the topping over the fruit in the pie plate.

Bake in the preheated oven for 30 minutes, or until the topping is golden brown.

Serve Mango-Raspberry Crumble warm with vanilla ice cream or whipped topping.

Makes 8 servings

Cost $4.91

FRUGAL FACT: *Look for online manufacturer's coupons for fresh berries during the height of the berry season in June and July. Pair the coupon with the sale price and get a pint or quart of fresh berries for as little as free to $.50.*

FREEZER FRIENDLY

Peach-Blueberry Crumble

1 pint blueberries ($1)
4 peaches, pitted and diced ($1.50)
½ cup brown sugar ($.12)

½ teaspoon ground cinnamon ($.03)
2 tablespoons all-purpose flour ($.02)

TOPPING

⅔ cup all-purpose flour ($.16)
½ cup quick-cooking oats ($.12)
⅓ cup brown sugar ($.05)

⅓ cup granulated sugar ($.04)
½ cup cold butter, cut into ½-inch
   chunks ($.80)

Ice cream or whipped topping ($.50)

Preheat the oven to 350 degrees. Grease an 8 × 8-inch glass baking dish with nonstick cooking spray.

Gently toss the blueberries, diced peaches, brown sugar, cinnamon, and flour in the prepared baking dish.

In a small mixing bowl, combine the flour, oats, and both sugars. Cut the butter pieces into the dry ingredients with a pastry blender or fork until the mixture is crumbly. Pour the topping over the fruit in the baking dish.

Bake in the preheated oven for 30 minutes, or until the topping is golden brown.

Serve Peach-Blueberry Crumble warm with vanilla ice cream or whipped topping.

Makes 8 servings

Cost $4.34

FRUGAL FACT: *Look for prices as low as $.49 per pound on peaches during the summer months. When they hit their rock-bottom prices, buy a few extra pounds and slice or dice them up and freeze. Frozen peaches are perfect for smoothies and for fruity desserts like this crumble.*

FREEZER FRIENDLY

Apple-Berry Crumble

2 Golden Delicious apples, peeled and cut into ½-inch chunks ($.50)

1 pint blueberries ($1)

½ pound strawberries, hulled and quartered ($1)

2½ tablespoons sugar ($.02)

1 teaspoon lemon juice ($.02)

TOPPING

1 cup quick-cooking oats ($.24)

1 cup all-purpose flour ($.20)

½ cup granulated sugar ($.05)

2 teaspoons ground cinnamon ($.10)

¼ teaspoon ground nutmeg ($.03)

½ cup butter or margarine ($.80)

Ice cream or whipped topping ($.50)

Preheat the oven to 350 degrees. Grease a 7 × 11-inch or 8 × 8-inch glass baking dish with nonstick cooking spray.

Gently toss the apples, blueberries, and strawberries with the sugar and lemon juice in the prepared baking dish.

In a small mixing bowl, mix together the oats, flour, sugar, cinnamon, and nutmeg. Using a pastry blender or fork, cut the butter or margarine into the dry ingredients until crumbles form. Pour the crumbles over the fruit in the baking dish.

Bake in the preheated oven for 30 minutes, or until the topping is golden brown.

Serve Apple-Berry Crumble with vanilla ice cream or whipped topping.

Makes 6 to 8 servings

Cost $4.44

FRUGAL FACT: *Bake this in a disposable baking dish, then let cool completely. Cover with aluminum foil and freeze. Then you've got dessert in the freezer to give to a friend in need of a tasty, sweet treat.*

FREEZER FRIENDLY

Pear-Apple Crisp

3 Anjou pears, peeled, cored and diced ($1)

3 Golden Delicious apples, peeled, cored, and diced ($.75)

½ cup brown sugar ($.12)

1 tablespoon all-purpose flour ($.01)

1 teaspoon ground cinnamon ($.05)

1 tablespoon lemon juice ($.05)

3 tablespoons butter, cut into ½-inch pieces ($.30)

TOPPING

1 cup quick-cooking oats ($.24)

½ cup brown sugar ($.12)

1 teaspoon ground cinnamon ($.05)

1 teaspoon ground nutmeg ($.10)

½ teaspoon salt

½ cup cold butter, cut into ½-inch pieces ($.75)

Ice cream or whipped topping ($.50)

Preheat the oven to 350 degrees. Grease an 8×8-inch glass baking dish with nonstick cooking spray.

Gently toss the pears, apples, sugar, flour, cinnamon, and lemon juice in the prepared baking dish, until the fruit is well coated with the dry ingredients.

In a small mixing bowl, combine the oats, sugar, cinnamon, nutmeg, and salt. Cut the butter pieces into the dry ingredients with a pastry blender or fork until the mixture is crumbly. Pour the topping over the fruit in the baking dish.

Bake in the preheated oven for 30 minutes, or until the topping is golden brown.

Serve Pear-Apple Crisp warm with vanilla ice cream or whipped topping.

Makes 8 servings

Cost $4.64

FRUGAL FACT: *The fruit mixture can be prepared in bulk and frozen in a plastic freezer bag or airtight freezer container. When you are ready to use it, thaw it in the refrigerator overnight, place in the baking dish, add the topping, and bake as directed.*

FREEZER FRIENDLY

Strawberry-Rhubarb Cobbler

1 pound strawberries ($2)

2 rhubarb stalks, 12- to 14-inches long, sliced crosswise ($.75)

¼ cup sugar ($.05)

½ teaspoon ground cinnamon ($.03)

1 teaspoon cornstarch ($.01)

TOPPING

1½ cups all-purpose flour ($.30)

¼ cup sugar ($.03)

2 teaspoons baking powder ($.10)

½ teaspoon salt

1 egg ($.10)

½ cup milk ($.05)

¼ cup butter, melted ($.40)

1 teaspoon vanilla extract ($.05)

Ice cream or whipped topping ($.50)

Preheat the oven to 375 degrees. Grease a 2-quart casserole dish, or 7 × 11-inch glass baking dish, with nonstick cooking spray.

Gently toss the strawberries, rhubarb slices, sugar, cinnamon, and cornstarch in the prepared baking dish.

In a small mixing bowl, combine the flour, sugar, baking powder, and salt. Whisk in the egg, milk, melted butter, and vanilla. Pour the batter over the fruit in the baking dish. Place the baking dish on a rimmed baking sheet to catch any juices that might bubble over.

Bake in the preheated oven for 40 to 45 minutes until the topping is golden brown.

Serve warm Strawberry-Rhubarb Cobbler with vanilla ice cream or whipped topping.

Makes 8 servings

Cost $4.37

FRUGAL FACT: *If you wish to make the fruit filling ahead and freeze it, do not include the cornstarch in the mixture. The cornstarch will turn mealy after it thaws. Just write on the plastic freezer bag that you need to add the cornstarch after the fruit thaws. You can also write the topping recipe onto the freezer bag so you don't have to get the cookbook out again.*

FREEZER FRIENDLY

Spiced Pear Bread Pudding

2 Anjou pears, peeled, cored, and diced ($.67)

½ cup granulated sugar ($.12)

1 teaspoon ground cinnamon ($.05)

1 teaspoon ground nutmeg ($.10)

1 teaspoon ground cloves ($.05)

2 cups day-old bread, cubed with crust removed ($.99)

2 eggs ($.20)

2 cups milk ($.20)

1 teaspoon vanilla extract ($.05)

¼ cup brown sugar ($.06)

Ice cream or whipped topping ($.50)

Grease an 8 × 8-inch glass baking dish with nonstick cooking spray.

Gently toss the diced pears, sugar, cinnamon, nutmeg, and ground cloves in the prepared baking dish. Then toss with the bread cubes.

In a small mixing bowl, whisk together the eggs, milk, vanilla, and brown sugar. Pour over the pear and bread mixture in the baking dish. Cover with plastic wrap and refrigerate for at least 2 hours, or overnight.

Preheat the oven to 400 degrees.

Remove the plastic wrap and bake the pudding in the preheated oven for 10 minutes. Reduce the oven temperature to 350 degrees and bake for another 20 to 25 minutes until a knife inserted in the center comes out clean.

Serve Spiced Pear Bread Pudding warm with vanilla ice cream or whipped topping.

Makes 8 servings

Cost $2.99

FRUGAL FACT: *If you can't manage to use up that day-old bread and still don't have time to make a dessert, pull it apart into chunks and then freeze in a plastic freezer bag. Save the bread chunks to use in this recipe, or other bread pudding or breakfast casserole recipes.*

One-Bowl Mocha Brownies

....

2 ounces semisweet baking chocolate, chopped ($.75)

½ cup butter ($.80)

2 cups chocolate chips, divided ($.99)

1 cup sugar ($.10)

1 teaspoon vanilla ($.03)

½ cup all-purpose flour ($.10)

2 tablespoons cocoa powder ($.06)

½ teaspoon salt

2 eggs ($.20)

1 packet (or 1 tablespoon) instant coffee granules ($.50)

Preheat the oven to 350 degrees. Grease an 8 × 8-inch glass baking dish with nonstick cooking spray.

In a large, microwave-safe mixing bowl, add the chopped baking chocolate, butter, and 1 cup of the chocolate chips. Microwave on high for 1½ minutes. Whisk the melted butter into the melted chocolate.

Whisk the sugar, vanilla, flour, cocoa powder, and salt into the butter-chocolate mixture. Whisk the eggs and instant coffee granules into the batter. Whisk for about 1 minute, or until the batter is smooth. Fold in the remaining 1 cup chocolate chips.

Pour the batter into the greased baking dish. Bake in the preheated oven for 25 to 30 minutes until a toothpick inserted in the center comes out clean. Let cool slightly before cutting and serving.

Makes 12 brownies

Cost $3.53

FRUGAL FACT: *Coupons for chocolate chips generally come out during the holidays, so be sure to get as many coupons as you can and stock up on these sweet little gems. Sealed bags of chocolate chips can be stored in the freezer for up to 1 year.*

FREEZER FRIENDLY

Nutty Butter Brownies

4 ounces semisweet baking chocolate, chopped ($1.49)

⅓ cup butter, softened ($.53)

¼ cup natural peanut butter ($.25)

1½ cups chocolate chips, divided ($.75)

1 cup sugar ($.10)

1 teaspoon vanilla extract ($.05)

1 egg ($.10)

½ cup all-purpose flour ($.10)

1 tablespoon cocoa powder ($.03)

¾ teaspoon baking powder ($.03)

½ teaspoon salt

1 cup mixed nuts, chopped ($1)

Preheat the oven to 350 degrees. Grease an 8 × 8-inch glass baking dish with nonstick cooking spray.

To a large, microwave-safe mixing bowl, add the chopped semisweet baking chocolate, butter, peanut butter, and 1 cup of the chocolate chips. Microwave on high for 1½ minutes. Whisk to combine.

Whisk in the sugar, vanilla, and egg into the chocolate mixture. Add the flour, cocoa powder, baking powder, and salt. Whisk until a batter forms.

Fold in the remaining chocolate chips and chopped mixed nuts. Pour the batter into the prepared baking dish.

Bake in the preheated oven for 25 to 30 minutes, or until a toothpick inserted in the center comes out clean. Let cool slightly before cutting and serving.

Serve Nutty Butter Brownies.

Makes 12 brownies

Cost $4.43

FRUGAL FACT: *If you use regular, sweetened peanut butter, reduce the sugar from 1 cup to ¾ cup.*

FREEZER FRIENDLY

Almond-Crusted Chocolate Chip Cookie Bars

....

2 cups chopped almonds ($1.50)

1¼ cups brown sugar, divided ($.20)

1 cup butter ($1.60)

¾ cup granulated sugar ($.08)

1 egg ($.10)

1 teaspoon vanilla extract ($.05)

1 cup whole wheat flour ($.28)

½ cup all-purpose flour ($.10)

1 teaspoon baking powder ($.05)

1 teaspoon salt

2 cups chocolate chips ($.99)

Preheat the oven to 350 degrees. Grease a 9 × 13-inch glass baking dish with nonstick cooking spray.

Spread the chopped almonds in the bottom of the prepared baking dish. Sprinkle ½ cup of the brown sugar over the almonds.

In a mixing bowl, beat together the butter, the remaining ¾ cup brown sugar, granulated sugar, egg, and vanilla until creamy. Add the wheat flour, all-purpose flour, baking powder, and salt. Beat until a dough forms, then fold in the chocolate chips.

Spread the cookie dough over the chopped almonds in the bottom of the baking dish. Wet your fingers with cold water and press the dough over the bottom of the dish and into the corners without displacing the chopped almonds.

Bake in the preheated oven for 25 to 30 minutes, or until a toothpick inserted in the center comes out clean. Let cool slightly before cutting and serving.

Serve Almond-Crusted Chocolate Chip Cookie Bars upside down.

Makes 24 bars

Cost $4.95

FRUGAL FACT: *Store almonds, walnuts, pecans, and other nuts in the freezer for up to 1 year.*

FREEZER FRIENDLY

One-Bowl Chewy Oatmeal Raisin Cookies

½ cup butter, softened ($.80)

1 cup brown sugar ($.25)

1 egg ($.10)

1 teaspoon vanilla extract ($.05)

1 cup all-purpose flour ($.20)

1 teaspoon ground cinnamon ($.05)

½ teaspoon ground nutmeg ($.05)

½ teaspoon baking soda ($.02)

½ teaspoon salt

1½ cups old-fashioned oats ($.18)

1 cup raisins ($.75)

Preheat the oven to 350 degrees. Grease a large baking sheet with nonstick cooking spray.

In a large mixing bowl, beat the butter and brown sugar with a hand mixer, or in the bowl of a stand mixer, until creamy. Add the egg and vanilla and beat to incorporate. Add the flour, cinnamon, nutmeg, baking soda, and salt and beat until the batter forms.

With the mixer on low speed, beat in the oats and raisins. Spoon 1½ tablespoons of dough about 2 inches apart onto the greased baking sheet and press lightly to flatten.

Bake in the preheated oven for 10 to 12 minutes, or until the cookies are baked through in the middle and begin to golden.

Serve One-Bowl Chewy Oatmeal Raisin Cookies.

Makes 2 dozen chewy cookies

Cost $2.45

FRUGAL FACT: *My "never-pay-more-than" price for an 18-ounce canister of old-fashioned oats is $.50.*

FREEZER FRIENDLY

TWELVE

Homemade Recipes for One-Dish Dinners

Homemade Chicken Stock

Leftover whole chicken carcass or leftover chicken bones or other chicken parts, such as the neck or back
Water

1 onion, chopped ($.30)
2 celery stalks, chopped ($.20)
2 garlic cloves ($.10)
Whole black peppercorns

Add the chicken carcass, pieces, and/or bones to a large pot along with the chopped onion, celery, garlic, and peppercorns.

Cover with at least 1 inch of water and bring to a boil. Reduce the heat, cover, and simmer over low heat for 2 hours.

Remove the stock from the heat and let cool. Strain out the chicken pieces and bones. Let the stock cool completely before freezing.

Freeze the chicken stock in freezer ziplock bags or small 1- or 2-cup-portion plastic, freezer-safe containers. Leave some air space in the baggie or container, as the stock will expand as it freezes.

Approximately 6 cups

Cost $.60 for approximately 6 cups, or $.10 per cup

FRUGAL FACT: *Stock can be partially thawed in a bowl of water in the refrigerator, then added to a pot to finish thawing.*

Homemade Beef Broth

3 to 4 pounds bone-in, beef roast
2 cups water
1 onion, quartered ($.30)

2 carrots ($.20)
2 potatoes, peeled and quartered
($.30)

Add the beef roast and 2 cups of water to the insert of a slow cooker. Add the onions, carrots, and potatoes around the beef roast. Set the slow cooker on low, and cook the roast for 8 hours.

When the meat has finished cooking, remove the roast and serve as a meal with the onions, carrots, and potatoes.

Strain the juices from the slow cooker and let the broth cool completely before freezing.

Freeze the beef broth in freezer ziplock bags or small 1- or 2-cup-portion plastic, freezer-safe containers. Leave some air space in the bag or container, as the stock will expand as it freezes.

Since you use the beef and vegetables in other recipes or meals, I'm going to say that this broth is "free" since all you're adding is water.

Makes 4 to 6 cups

Cost $.20 per cup

FRUGAL FACT: *If you want smaller portions than the recommended 1- or 2- cup portions, freeze the broth in ice cube trays, then transfer the cubes to freezer ziplock bags once they are frozen. Each cube yields 2 to 3 tablespoons of stock or broth.*

Homemade Vegetable Stock

2 cups of leftover vegetables or
  peelings (see Frugal Fact) ($.50)
6 cups water

2 teaspoons freshly ground black
  pepper
1 bay leaf ($.05)

Wash and rinse all the vegetables, peelings, and other vegetable parts. Add to large saucepan and add water, pepper, and bay leaf.

Simmer the stock for 1 hour. Remove from heat and let cool. Strain off any vegetable pieces. Let the stock cool completely before freezing.

Freeze the vegetable stock in plastic freezer bags or small 1- or 2-cup-portion plastic containers. Leave some air space in the baggie or container, as the stock will expand as it freezes.

Makes approximately 6 cups

Cost $.55 for approximately 6 cups, or $.09/cup

FRUGAL FACT: *This is a great way to use up vegetable pieces or whole vegetables that otherwise might be thrown out. Suggested vegetables and their peelings to use when making vegetable stock: potatoes, sweet potatoes, onions, garlic, carrots, celery, peas, empty corn cobs, green beans, green onions, and herbs. Asparagus, tomatoes, broccoli, and cauliflower tend to be overpowering flavors in the stock, but do not have to be avoided.*

Homemade Pizza Sauce

1 can (15 ounces) tomato sauce ($.59)   1 teaspoon garlic powder ($.05)

1 teaspoon dried oregano ($.05)   1 teaspoon onion powder ($.05)

1 teaspoon dried basil ($.05)   2 teaspoons extra-virgin olive oil ($.05)

In a small saucepan or skillet, whisk the tomato sauce with the spices and olive oil. Simmer for 6 to 8 minutes.

Makes 2 cups

Cost for 2 cups $.84

Homemade Salsa Fresca (Fresh Salsa)

6 large tomatoes ($2)

2 Serrano chiles ($.79)

3 garlic cloves, crushed ($.15)

½ onion, quartered ($.15)

2 teaspoons olive oil ($.05)

Quarter the tomatoes and place in a food processor or blender.

Cut the stems off the chiles. Remove some seeds if you prefer a milder salsa. Add the chiles, crushed garlic, quartered onions, and olive oil to the food processor or blender.

Blend or puree until the salsa reaches the desired consistency.

Serve the salsa with chips, or use when cooking or in recipes that call for salsa, like Mexican Pizza Bites (page 82) and Southwest Chicken Chili (page 190).

Makes 2 to 3 cups

Cost for 2 to 3 cups $3.04

FRUGAL FACT: *If you don't have space for a garden, consider growing a hot pepper plant in a medium pot on an outdoor table.*

Homemade Dressings

Making your own dressing is just plain healthier than using store-bought dressings. Your own dressings are preservative-free and taste fresher. I bet you'd be surprised that you have most of the ingredients in your pantry or refrigerator already.

Homemade Basic Vinaigrette

¼ cup vinegar ($.20)
½ cup extra-virgin olive oil ($.40)
1 teaspoon lemon juice ($.02)
1 garlic clove, crushed ($.05)

1 teaspoon sugar ($.01)
1 teaspoon dried basil ($.05)
Salt and pepper

In a small bottle or plastic container, shake the vinegar, olive oil, lemon juice, garlic, sugar, basil, and salt and pepper to taste.

Makes ¾ cup dressing

Cost $.73

Homemade Balsamic Vinaigrette

....

4 tablespoons balsamic vinegar ($.25)   1 garlic clove, crushed ($.05)
½ cup extra-virgin olive oil ($.40)   Salt and pepper

In a small bottle or plastic container, shake the vinegar, olive oil, garlic, and salt and pepper to taste.

Makes ¾ cup dressing

Cost $.70

Homemade Dijon Vinaigrette

....

3 tablespoons vinegar ($.15)   2 tablespoons Dijon mustard ($.10)
½ cup extra-virgin olive oil ($.40)   Salt and pepper

In a small bottle or plastic container, shake the vinegar, olive oil, Dijon mustard, and salt and pepper to taste.

Makes ⅔ cup dressing

Cost $.65

Homemade Whole Wheat Pizza Dough

1 cup lukewarm water

2 cups all-purpose flour ($.28)

1 packet active dry yeast ($.25)

1 tablespoon sugar ($.01)

1 teaspoon salt

1 tablespoon extra-virgin olive
oil ($.05)

1 cup whole wheat flour ($.25)

1 teaspoon dried Italian
seasoning ($.05)

2 tablespoons grated Parmesan cheese
($.10)

Olive oil and garlic salt (optional)

BY-HAND DIRECTIONS

In a mixing bowl, combine the lukewarm water and 1 cup of the all-purpose flour. Add the yeast, sugar, salt, and oil. Whisk together to make a "spongy" dough. Let sit for 10 to 15 minutes.

Add the remaining 2 cups of flour to the sponge and stir with a wooden spoon. When the dough becomes thick enough, knead it by hand for 6 to 8 minutes on a floured surface or in a floured bowl until it reaches the consistency of soft baby skin. Knead the seasonings and cheese into the dough. Place in a floured or greased bowl and let rise for 45 minutes to 1 hour.

Once the dough has risen and doubled in size, the dough is ready to be formed. Place the dough on a lightly floured work surface. Sprinkle flour over the dough and on the rolling pin. Roll out the dough to the desired size.

Brush the edges of the dough with olive oil and sprinkle with garlic salt, if desired.

Bake the crust for 8 minutes, remove from oven, and load with toppings. Bake the full pizza 8 to 10 minutes more. Slice and serve.

BREAD MACHINE DIRECTIONS

Add the water and olive oil to the bread machine bowl. Add the whole wheat and white flours. With a spoon, create a well in the flour for the yeast. Add the yeast into the well, being careful not to let the yeast touch any water.

Add the sugar, Italian seasoning, cheese, and salt.

Set the bread machine to the dough cycle.

Once the dough has formed in the bread machine, carefully remove it and place it on a lightly floured counter. Sprinkle flour over the dough and on the rolling pin. Roll out the dough to the desired size.

This recipe will make two 8-inch thin-crust pizzas, four 4-inch deep dish pizza crusts, or one 16-inch thick-crust pizza.

Brush the edges of the dough with olive oil and sprinkle with garlic salt, if desired.

Bake the crust for 8 minutes, remove from the oven, and load with the toppings. Bake the full pizza 8 to 10 minutes more. Slice and serve.

Makes 1 14-inch pizza crust

Cost $.92

FRUGAL FACT: *Involve young children in the pizza dough–making process. It might be messy, but will create warm memories in both yours and your children's minds!*

Homemade Mashed Potatoes "Ratio"

....

4 medium Idaho potatoes ($.60)   1 teaspoon onion powder ($.05)

4 tablespoons butter ($.40)   ½ teaspoon salt

½ cup milk or light sour cream ($.05)   ½ teaspoon pepper

1 teaspoon garlic powder ($.05)

Peel, quarter, and boil the potatoes for 10 minutes. Drain the potatoes and return them to the pan. Add the butter, milk or sour cream, garlic powder, onion powder, and salt and pepper.

Mash with a potato masher until you reach the desired consistency. Add more milk, ¼ cup at a time, for creamier mashed potatoes.

Makes 4 portions

Cost $1.15 using the ratio recipe above

FRUGAL FACT: *Prepared mashed potatoes can be frozen in 2- or 4-cup portions. Thaw quickly in a warm bowl of water.*

Homemade Taco Seasoning

1 part chili powder
1 part ground cumin
1 part garlic powder

1 part onion powder
¼ to ½ part crushed red pepper
  flakes

Mix all the spices together and store in an airtight container in the cupboard or freezer.

Ratio recipe: amount varies

Cost $.60 if using 1 tablespoon per part

FRUGAL FACT: *Look for sales on the different spice ingredients at the national drugstores chains. Don't pay more than $.75 for a 1- to 2-ounce container of spices.*

Homemade Pie Crust

1 cup all-purpose flour ($.20)

½ teaspoon salt

⅓ cup shortening or butter ($.50)

½ teaspoon cold white vinegar ($.01)

3 to 4 tablespoons cold water

In a medium mixing bowl, combine the flour and salt and then cut in the butter or shortening, until crumbles form.

Using a fork, toss in the vinegar and 2 tablespoons of the cold water. Toss together until dough starts to come together. Add more water 1 tablespoon at a time. Gently knead as the dough ball forms.

Place the dough onto a clean, flat, lightly floured surface and roll it out into a circle. Transfer the pie crust to a pie plate.

Makes 1 pie crust

Cost $.71

FRUGAL FACT: *Homemade pie crust can be made in batches and frozen in the shape of the pie crust, or gently rolled up with wax paper or parchment paper and then placed in plastic freezer bags.*

Grilled Garlic Bread

1 loaf French bread, or slices of
    sandwich bread ($.49)
Butter or margarine, amount will
    vary depending on loaf size ($.25)

Garlic salt ($.05)
Black pepper
Parmesan cheese (optional) ($.10)

Slice the French loaf bread open horizontally. Spread the butter on the bread, then sprinkle the garlic salt and pepper and Parmesan cheese, if you prefer. Then spread the butter again, to ensure that the spices or cheese do not fall into the grill.

Place the buttered side of the bread facedown over indirect heat on the grill. Grill for 3 to 5 minutes. The grilling time will depend on the heat level of your grill. You want the bread to be slightly crispy and the butter melted.

Makes 4 bread servings

Cost $.79 to $.89

FRUGAL FACT: *Grilled garlic bread is the perfect way to revive an almost stale loaf of bread, or a loaf of bread from the freezer that you purchased on a manager's special.*

Homemade Stuffing

10 slices loaf bread ($.69)

1 teaspoon poultry seasoning ($.05)

½ teaspoon garlic powder ($.03)

½ teaspoon onion powder ($.03)

½ teaspoon salt

½ teaspoon pepper

Preheat the oven to 225 degrees.

Cut the bread slices into ½-inch pieces and lay out flat on a rimmed baking sheet. Place in the preheated oven for 45 minutes to 1 hour until all the bread pieces have dried out.

Remove from the oven and let cool completely. Once cooled, slide the dried bread pieces into a large mixing bowl and toss with the poultry seasoning, garlic powder, onion powder, salt and pepper.

Store in an airtight container.

Makes about 4 cups stuffing mix

Cost $.80

FRUGAL FACT: *Homemade stuffing mix can be prepared and then frozen in a plastic freezer bag, once it has completely cooled.*

APPENDIX A

Pantry Staples List

Another aspect of saving money and time when planning and making meals is having an organized and fully stocked kitchen. By having "the basic" ingredients in my stockpile, I don't find myself thinking "I just don't have anything to cook today," and grabbing the keys to head out for a fast-food lunch.

Below are my recommendations for the "must-haves" in the freezer, refrigerator, pantry, and other cooking and baking supplies.

Freezer

Chicken breasts
Ground beef

Ground turkey
Fresh or frozen fish

Shrimp

Any favorite meat cuts that are reduced for quick sale and not to be used immediately

Frozen vegetables

Frozen fruit

Breads that are reduced for quick sale and not to be used immediately

Homemade beef broth, chicken stock, or vegetable stock

Precooked Ingredients

1-pound portions of browned ground beef

2-cup portions of cooked, shredded chicken

1½-pound portions of meatballs, uncooked

2-cup portions of grilled chicken slices

2-cup portions of diced grilled chicken

2-cup portions of cooked dried beans of all varieties

Cooked bacon, in slices and crumbles

Cooked sausage in crumbles, slices, or links

Make-Ahead Meal Packets and Frozen Casseroles are noted on appropriate recipes

Refrigerator

Milk

Eggs

Cheese: sliced, bar, shredded, grated*

Deli meats

Butter or margarine

Yogurt

Fresh fruits

Fresh vegetables

Ketchup

Mustard

Mayonnaise

Sandwich spread

Vinegar—white, cider, balsamic, red wine, white wine

Natural peanut butter

Natural jelly

Pickles

* Notes freezer-friendly food

Baking

All-purpose flour
Wheat flour
Baking powder
Baking soda
Salt
Baking cocoa
Granulated sugar
Brown sugar

Powdered sugar
Honey
Stevia
Shortening
Oil: vegetable, canola, extra-virgin
    olive oil, pure olive oil
Flavored extracts, including vanilla
Flaxseed*

Pantry/Cupboard

Breads: sandwich bread, bagels,
    English muffins, pita bread,
    French loaf bread, buns*
Tortillas: flour, corn, whole wheat*
Dried beans
Variety of canned beans, if not
    cooking dried beans
White rice
Brown rice
Variety of pasta: white and whole
    wheat

Pasta sauces
Tomato sauce
Tomato paste
Variety of canned tomatoes
Jarred or canned salsa
Green chilies
Canned tuna
Beef, chicken, vegetable broth, if not
    making homemade

* Notes freezer-friendly food

Herbs and Spices

Kosher salt

Cracked pepper

Creole seasoning

Crushed red pepper flakes

Basil

Oregano

Thyme

Rosemary

Italian seasoning

Minced onion

Garlic powder

Garlic salt

Onion powder

Ground cumin

Chili powder

Ground ginger

Ground cloves

Allspice

Ground nutmeg

Pumpkin pie spice

Poultry seasoning

Dill

Paprika

Lemon pepper

Seafood seasoning

Other Cooking Supplies

Aluminum foil

Plastic wrap

Plastic freezer bags

Napkins

Paper towels

APPENDIX B

Essential Kitchen Gadgets

By utilizing certain electronic kitchen appliances and kitchen gadgets, time will be saved and frustrations reduced in the preparation of meals. Below are my recommendations for "must-haves" in the kitchen drawers and on the countertop for making One-Dish Dinners.

Small Appliances

Slow cooker

Bread machine

Blender or food processor

Mini chopper

Stand mixer or hand mixer

Baking Essentials

Mixing bowls

Measuring cups and spoons

Mixing and serving spoons

Spatulas

Plastic scrapers

Baking sheets

Square and rectangular glass baking
dishes

For the Stove

Dutch oven or stockpot

Small, medium, and large saucepans

Cast-iron skillet

Skillet, frying pan, or sauté pan

Stovetop steamer

Handy Gadgets

Cheese grater

Garlic press

Slotted serving spoons

Wooden spoons

Kitchen shears

Chef's knife

Paring knife

Plastic and wood cutting boards

APPENDIX C

Online Resources

T oday there exist hundreds, if not thousands, of resources on the internet that help consumers save money, including my Web sites www.onedish dinners.com or www.5dollardinners.com. The site is updated on a daily basis with resources for meal planning, couponing, and strategic grocery shopping.

Below is a list of Web sites where coupons can be printed directly from the site, as well as information on how to find a blogger in your area who shares coupon matchups for your store, plus where to find details on recommended daily food requirements.

Couponing Resources

www.coupons.com

www.smartsource.com

www.redplum.com

www.couponnetwork.com

www.couponmom.com

www.mambosprouts.com/coupons (organic coupons)

www.foodallergiesonabudget.com (allergy-free food coupons)

GROCERY STORE COUPON MATCHUPS

Also, hundreds of bloggers post coupon matchups each week for hundreds of different stores across the country. To find a blogger in your local area who offers this free service, simply *Google* your city's name and the phrase "grocery store coupon matchups." This will lead you to the blogger who has already done the coupon matchups for the grocery stores in your area each week.

By taking the time to explore these great online resources and make grocery lists and meal plans based on the sale items and coupon matchups, you are sure to start reducing your weekly grocery bill.

PORTION SIZES AND RECOMMENDED DAILY FOOD REQUIREMENTS

www.mypyramid.gov/mypyramid/index.aspx

INDEX